CONTENTS BY THEME

Church Seasons and Festivals   **Openings 1–21**

Special Celebrations   **Openings 22–29**

Church Symbols and Words   **Openings 30–49**

Life in Bible Times   **Openings 50–61**

Church Heroes/Cont

Find It in the Bible

Local and Global Miss   Openings 90–101

MW01045752

CHECKLIST OF OPENINGS BY TITLE

Record the date of usage on the line following each title.

An asterisk (*) denotes openings that especially need advance planning.

1 Church Seasons I _____	*35 Eternal Life _____	*69 Corrie ten Boom _____
2 Church Seasons II _____	36 Faith _____	70 Mother Teresa _____
3 Church Seasons III _____	37 Forgiveness _____	71 Martin Luther King Jr. _____
4 Advent I _____	38 Holy Communion _____	72 Desmond Tutu _____
*5 Advent II _____	39 Holy Spirit _____	73 Robert Hill _____
6 Christmas I _____	40 Lamb of God _____	74 Joni Eareckson Tada _____
7 Christmas II _____	41 The Lord's Prayer _____	75 Kathryn Koob _____
*8 Christmas III _____	42 Love _____	76 Hometown Heroes _____
9 Christmas IV _____	43 Peace _____	77 God's Word I _____
10 Epiphany I _____	44 Prayer _____	78 God's Word II _____
*11 Epiphany II _____	45 Resurrection _____	79 Testaments _____
12 Epiphany III _____	46 Sheep and Shepherds _____	80 Old Testament _____
13 Ash Wednesday _____	47 Stewardship _____	81 New Testament _____
14 Lent I _____	*48 Thanksgiving _____	82 Chapter:Verse I _____
15 Lent II _____	49 Trinity _____	83 Chapter:Verse II _____
16 Holy Week I _____	50 Holy Land _____	84 Types of Writing _____
17 Holy Week II _____	*51 Shepherds _____	85 Law _____
18 Easter I _____	52 Foods _____	86 Good News _____
19 Easter II _____	53 Bread _____	87 Songs _____
20 Pentecost I _____	54 Water _____	88 Bible Game I _____
*21 Pentecost II _____	55 Houses _____	89 Bible Game II _____
22 Rally Day _____	56 Hospitality _____	90 World Prayer _____
*23 Celebrating Friendship _____	57 Occupations _____	91 Our Project _____
24 Celebrating Our Church _____	58 Clothing _____	92 Missionary Visitors _____
*25 Creation Celebration _____	59 Music _____	*93 Discovering Needs _____
26 World Day _____	60 The Temple _____	94 World Hunger _____
27 Celebrating Children _____	61 The Sabbath _____	95 Group Adoption _____
28 All Saints' Day _____	62 Athanasius _____	96 Empty Bags _____
29 Passover _____	63 Martin Luther _____	*97 Love Kits _____
30 Angels _____	64 Johann Sebastian Bach _____	98 Love Tape _____
31 Baptism _____	65 Mary Jones _____	*99 Collection Sunday _____
32 Christian _____	66 Harriet Tubman _____	100 Church Servants _____
33 Church _____	67 Toyohiko Kagawa _____	101 Church Welcome _____
34 Cross _____	68 Mary McLeod Bethune _____	

USING THIS RESOURCE

If you lead church school openings for elementary-aged students, then this book was written especially for you. Each opening is a mini-lesson, lasting 10 to 15 minutes and covering topics that may not be included in your church school curriculum: Church Seasons and Festivals, Special Celebrations, Church Symbols and Words, Life in Bible Times, Church Heroes/Contemporary Heroes, Find It in the Bible, and Local and Global Mission. The openings can also be used to introduce, expand upon, and review topics that are covered by the curriculum.

Learner involvement is a key ingredient. Students have an opportunity to learn from one another as they hear, experience, and share the good news. Through cooperative interaction, students of different ages learn what it means to be part of God's family.

As you think about the place where the openings will be held, ask the following questions: How can things be arranged to allow the space needed? How can a pleasant atmosphere be achieved? Are there any safety issues to be addressed? Is it accessible to students with special needs? Several openings contain games or simulation activities that require a large open area. Can your space accommodate this, or will adaptations or alternate sites be needed?

Cooperation with church school teachers is essential. The ideal situation is to have the church school teachers involved as active participants. That way they can relate what is being learned during the opening to what is being learned in class. Ask for their suggestions of topics they would like you to cover. A Scripture Index is included at the end of this book that will help you determine if there is an opening based on the Bible text of a specific class lesson. Warn the teachers in advance if you think an opening may last more than 15 minutes.

These openings are designed to provide the basic information needed for presentation. You may occasionally need to do a little additional reading or ask some questions of others if there are words or practices with which you are not familiar. Let it be a learning experience for you as well. It will be your decision as to what adaptation will be needed. Adjustments may be necessary if you have a very small or a very large group. You may decide that you need to use more simplified language and provide more background information in order for the students to grasp the idea. Remember that some may have limited experience with church vocabulary, concepts, or practices. Bring in additional materials, if available. Photographs, drawings, and objects bring life to a lesson. Write your ideas in the margins. Paper-clip your creative adaptations and follow-up activities into this book so you can remember them for future use.

Be flexible in your scheduling. Go where the students' enthusiasm leads. If they want to learn more about a topic, build on that interest. Give the students opportunities to see faith in action.

It is expected that music will be an important part of these openings. The selection of music is left to you or a music helper, allowing the usage of whatever music resources you have available or prefer. Continue to incorporate whatever traditions already exist, such as collecting the offering or celebrating birthdays during the opening.

Each opening includes a Bible text, preparation and presentation instructions, and a prayer. Some direct you to related openings. Others have suggestions for follow-up activities. Along with this recurring format, there are some general instructions that apply to all the openings. Be sure to review these general instructions before planning any openings.

MATERIALS TO HAVE AVAILABLE FOR EACH OPENING

1. A Bible.
2. A writing surface, such as a chalkboard or pad of chart paper, mounted where all the students can see it; and something with which to write.
3. A selection of colored markers and large sheets of paper, or poster board, for writing Bible texts, prayers, responsive readings, etc. You will also need tape, tacks, or a clothesline and clothespins for displaying these writings where the students can see them.
4. Many lessons require that objects be placed on a table in front of the students. Read through the opening you plan to do to determine what additional props will be needed. If your students will be sitting on the floor during openings, you will want to display items in a way that allows good visibility.

GENERAL PREPARATIONS FOR EACH OPENING

1. Read through the entire opening before beginning your preparations.
2. Find and read the Bible text. If you will be reading it to the students, practice reading it aloud to yourself. Mark the place in your Bible with a bookmark.
3. Pray as you prepare.
4. Include music that tells of God's love and offers praise to God for that love. Include a variety of styles, keeping in mind the musical abilities of the

group and their level of understanding. If you feel uncomfortable teaching or leading songs, arrange for someone to do it for you.

5. Some openings require preparations to be made several weeks in advance. Make plans accordingly. Some openings may extend beyond one session, depending upon the size of your group and how involved they become in certain parts. Think through each opening to determine if it should be split. If so, you may need to plan how you will bring the first half to a close and introduce the second half.

6. When the directions say "Write Micah 4:3 on a large sheet of paper," write out the verse word for word from the Bible. If the instructions tell you to write "Micah 4:3," write exactly what is printed between the quotation marks, not the words of the verse. When you are asked to write something, do so on the chalkboard or chart paper unless other instructions are given.

7. Always have a backup activity in case you have a few extra minutes. Some ideas are: Bible riddles, a song, a short game.

8. Be prepared and ready to begin on time.

PRESENTATION HINTS

1. Before the opening officially begins, chat with the students about their activities and interests.

2. Welcome the students at the beginning of each opening. Introduce yourself, or ask one of the students to introduce you. If time allows, introduce new students and guests.

3. Use student restlessness to help you pace the openings. You may have to cut a discussion short. If so, encourage those who are interested to see if they can continue the discussion in their class.

4. Many of these openings have information provided for generating and supplementing discussions. Let the students do most of the talking. If a student mentions something related to the provided information, add it to the discussion at that time. Once the students have shared everything they know about that topic, add any of the remaining information that you feel is necessary to complete the discussion.

5. Several of the openings in Church Seasons and Festivals ask you to make large calendars. Save any calendars you make since they may be reusable in another session.

6. When group work is called for, mix children of various ages and encourage interaction and cooperation.

7. Have fun. Enjoy yourself. Smile.

A glossary of church season colors, symbols, and definitions is found in Appendix A at the back of this book. You may want to refer to those pages frequently as you prepare for Openings 1–21.

CHURCH SEASONS I

TEXT   Psalm 47:1

PREPARATION   Refer to Appendix A as you prepare six felt or poster board banners which will be reused in several other openings. Make each the color of the church season it represents: Advent, sky blue or purple; Christmas, white; Epiphany, green; Lent, purple; Easter, white; and Pentecost, green. Label each banner with the name of the church season it represents. Make and attach one or more paper or felt symbols to each banner. Learn the meaning of each symbol chosen.

PRESENTATION

Ask the students to name the four seasons of the calendar year. (*Spring, summer, fall, winter.*) Ask if there are particular colors or objects they think of in connection with those seasons. (*Spring—pastel colors, flowers, bunnies; summer—yellow sun, beaches, picnics; fall—orange and gold, pumpkins, colored leaves, school buses; winter—white, snow, red and green, things related to Christmas.*) Say, "There is a special kind of calendar we use in the church. It isn't divided into months and weeks and days. It is divided into six parts that help us remember the things that happened in Jesus' life and the things he taught. We call this the church calendar, or the seasons of the church year."

Distribute the church season banners and invite the six volunteers to stand in a line, facing the other students. Have the banners displayed from left to right in the same order as they are listed in "Preparation." Read the names of the seasons together. As you point to each banner, ask the students to share what they know about each season. Provide additional information if clarification is needed. If you plan to use the next several openings, tell the students that they will be learning more about the individual seasons in the weeks to come. Read the Bible text.

PRAYER   "Lord, during each of the six seasons of the church year, help us to remember and celebrate all that you've done for us. Amen."

RELATED OPENINGS   2, 4, 7, 10, 14, 18, 20

SUGGESTED FOLLOW-UP   Keep these banners for use in several other openings.

CHURCH SEASONS II

2

TEXT   Ecclesiastes 3:1

PREPARATION   Draw each symbol used in Opening 1 on a separate sheet of paper. Write the following prayers on large sheets of paper: (1) Thank you, Lord, for Advent, when we prepare for Christmas and look forward to the time when you will come again. (2) Thank you, God, for Christmas, when we celebrate the birth of your Son Jesus. (3) Lord, thank you for Epiphany, a time to remember the gift of Baptism, a time to tell others the good news. (4) Lord, during Lent we thank you for the gift of Holy Communion. Thank you for dying on the cross so that our sins are forgiven. (5) Lord, we praise you for Easter and for giving us new life by raising Jesus from the dead. Thank you for the gift of eternal life. (6) At Pentecost we thank you, God, for the gift of the Holy Spirit. Keep us growing in faith. Amen.

Read the Bible text. Say, "The Christian church has divided the year into six seasons. Who can name some of them?" Once they've been named, say, "Today we're going to play a game. Each of you will be in a group, representing a church season. I'll show you a church season symbol. If it belongs to your season, everyone in your group should stand." Divide the students into six groups and assign each a church season. Hold up one symbol picture at a time. After each symbol has been claimed, invite someone to explain its meaning.

PRAYER Have each group read the numbered prayer that corresponds to the group's assigned season.

CHURCH SEASONS III ☐3☐

TEXT Deuteronomy 32:3

PREPARATION You will need a large open area. Bring 1½" x 3" self-adhesive labels, one per student. On each label, write the name of one of the church seasons. Prepare an equal number for each season. Stack the labels in sets of six, each set containing one of each of the church seasons. Create a rap by chanting the six seasons in chronological order (see Opening 1) so that they sound like a train chugging. Bring a stopwatch and a bell or whistle. Display the prayer posters mentioned in Opening 2. Invite some adults or teens to help. Learn the following rules for "Church Seasons Trains." Place a church season label on each person's back. Tell each person their season and ask that they remember it. If there are leftover seasons in one set, place the remaining labels on the backs of your helpers. Choose someone to be the timer. Tell them to begin timing on the signal and stop when the last train is complete. Have the students walk around the game area, rapping the names of the church seasons in unison. When they hear the signal (bell or whistle), they are to stop rapping and form trains by holding onto the waist of a person belonging to the church season that comes immediately before their season. Each train should have six people, with "Advent" in front and "Pentecost" at the back. Record the time. Play the game again. See if the students can improve their time.

PRESENTATION

Read the Bible text. Say, "The church seasons help us keep our minds and hearts on God. Who can name all six church seasons?" Have the students practice rapping the names of the church seasons so that they sound like a train. Explain how to play "Church Seasons Trains."

PRAYER Invite the students representing each church season to read the prayer poster that corresponds to their season.

ADVENT I ☐4☐

TEXT Micah 5:2

PREPARATION Make or reuse the Advent banner described in Opening 1. Make a large calendar showing the end of November and all of December. Write "St. Andrew's Day" on November 30 and "Christmas" on December 25. Gather some, or all, of the following: an Advent wreath, an Advent log, Jesse tree and ornaments, Advent calendar(s), and Advent devotional book(s).

PRESENTATION

Display the Advent banner. Ask the students to tell what they remember about Advent. Review the meaning of each symbol and the color (see Appendix A). Show them the calendar. Point to December 25 on the calendar and say, "This is when we celebrate Christmas. Advent is the time when we get ready for Christmas. Advent begins on the Sunday closest to St. Andrew's Day, November 30. There are four Sundays in Advent. (*Count them together on the calendar.*) The length of Advent varies from year to year." Engage the students in discussion about the preparations that take place in their homes before Christmas. Discuss Advent traditions and show the items you brought. Encourage the students to describe any Advent traditions they observe in their homes. Ask, "Why do we have a time of waiting before Christmas?" Discuss how God prepared the world for a Savior. God sent prophets who told the people that a Savior was coming. Read the Bible text. Ask, "What does this prophecy from the prophet Micah tell us?"

PRAYER   Invite the students to say, "Lord, prepare us" at each pause in the following prayer: "Lord, Christmas is coming *(pause)*. Be with us as we get ready to celebrate *(pause)*. Be with us as we look forward to the time when you will come again *(pause)*. Amen."

RELATED OPENING   80

ADVENT II 5

TEXTS   Isaiah 7:14; Micah 7:7

PREPARATION   Plan a breakfast to be served right after this opening. Invite some teens and/or adults to prepare, serve, and clean up after the breakfast. Plan a meal with delicious smells. Inform the students about this breakfast well in advance so they will have hearty appetites. Write Micah 7:7 on a large sheet of paper. Choose a table grace.

PRESENTATION

Ask, "What's happening after this opening? How can you tell? Did someone promise that there would be breakfast? You're waiting for breakfast. The people in Old Testament times waited for a Savior, someone who would save them from being punished for their sins. How did they know a Savior was coming? (*God's messengers, the prophets, promised them that a Savior would come.*)" Read Isaiah 7:14. "Was a Savior born? Who was the Savior? How do we know that Jesus came? (*We can read about his coming in the Bible.*) How do we know that Jesus will come again? (*The Bible tells us.*)" Point to Micah 7:7. Say, "Micah was a prophet. He wrote these words before the birth of Jesus, but they have meaning for us today." Read the Bible text together.

PRAYER   Sing, or say, the table grace.

SUGGESTED FOLLOW-UP   After breakfast, have centers where the students can make Advent banners, wreaths, logs, devotional books, etc.

CHRISTMAS I 6

TEXT   Luke 2:6-16

PREPARATION

Cut one strip of paper per student. Write "Mary" on one, "Joseph" on another, and "Angel of the Lord" on a third. On a third of the remaining strips, write "Shepherd."

On the others, write "Angel." Fold and place these strips in a container. On a large sheet of paper, write Luke 2:14. Write Luke 2:10b-12 on an index card. On a large sheet of paper, write "Fields." On another, write "Heaven." On a third, write "Inn." Label a box "Manger." Bring a doll and masking tape. Before the students arrive, place the "Inn" sign in a central location. Place the "Manger" nearby. Hide the doll behind the manger. Hang "Heaven" and "Fields" on opposite sides of your area. Place Luke 2:14 near "Fields."

PRESENTATION

As the students arrive, invite each one to choose a slip of paper. Ask two students to be Mary and Joseph. Ask a student who can read to be the Angel of the Lord. Give the Angel of the Lord the index card. Gather around the empty manger. Say, "Long ago there was a man named Francis. He lived in Assisi, Italy. His family had a lot of money and he could have had almost anything he wanted. But he gave away everything he owned when he was a young man. He spent the rest of his life as a poor man, telling others about Jesus. One winter evening near Christmas, Francis was traveling to a small town. On the way he saw shepherds out in the fields. They reminded him of the shepherds in the Bible story of Jesus' birth. That gave Francis an idea. He invited the townspeople to come to a nearby hillside on Christmas Eve. When they arrived, they saw people pretending to be Mary, Joseph, the baby in the manger, and the shepherds. There were real animals, too. As the people gazed in delight at the scene, Francis read them the story of Jesus' birth from the Bible. The people liked the scene so much that they created one every year. People in many parts of the world still create life-size scenes each Christmas. Others set up smaller scenes with nativity figures made of clay, wood, or other materials. Maybe you have a nativity set at home. Today we're going to create our own scene." Ask the Angels to stand "in Heaven," and the Shepherds to sit "in the Fields." Have Mary and Joseph kneel next to the Manger. Explain that after the Angel of the Lord talks to the shepherds, all the angels will go to the Fields and read their part from the large sheet of paper before returning to Heaven. Have the students act out the story as you read the Bible text.

PRAYER   Gather around the Manger. Invite prayer requests. Pray for their requests.

RELATED OPENINGS   30, 51, 75

SUGGESTED FOLLOW-UP   Set up a nativity set.

CHRISTMAS II

TEXT   Matthew 2:1a

PREPARATION   Make or reuse the Christmas banner described in Opening 1. Make a large calendar, showing December and January. Bring one large self-adhesive star and eleven smaller stars.

PRESENTATION

Read the Bible text. Display the calendar. Invite a volunteer to place the large star on Christmas Day. Ask, "How long is the Christmas season?" Count the 12 days of Christmas. Have students place one small star on each day of the Christmas season. Invite the students to share some ways they are going to celebrate the birth of Jesus during Christmas. Review the meaning of the symbols and the color on the banner.

PRAYER   "Lord, be with us as we celebrate your birth. Help us joyfully receive you as our Savior. Amen."

CHRISTMAS III

8

TEXT Luke 2:1-20

PREPARATION Several weeks in advance, assign each class a section of the Bible text to illustrate. Each class should make one large illustration. Collect them the week before this opening. Arrange them in the order they will be presented. Check with each teacher to see if a student volunteer would like to read the Bible text that goes with their illustration.

PRESENTATION

Show the first illustration. Read, or have the class volunteer read, the accompanying Bible text. Repeat with the other illustrations. Sing some of the students' favorite Christmas carols.

PRAYER "Lord, lead us to those people who haven't heard about Jesus. Help us tell them the good news. Amen."

RELATED OPENINGS 23, 75

CHRISTMAS IV

9

TEXT Isaiah 9:6

PREPARATION Festively wrap a large empty box. Write "Jesus" on an 8½" x 11" piece of paper. Fold and place this paper in a small box. Wrap it in plain brown paper. Display the two boxes on a table.

PRESENTATION

Invite the students to choose which package they would like to unwrap. If there is a difference of opinion, vote. Ask a volunteer to unwrap the chosen package. If the students opened the fancy package, ask them, "What did you expect? Are you disappointed?" Continue by saying, "Many people in Old Testament times looked forward to the Savior God had promised. What kind of a Savior do you think they expected?" Explain that they expected someone powerful and strong, the kind of person who would live in a palace. Then say, "We're like those Old Testament people. Most of us expect the best gifts to come in large, fancy packages. Who would have expected a baby Savior to be born in a stable?" Discuss why God might have sent a helpless, little baby Savior instead of a powerful adult; a Savior born to a carpenter and his wife instead of one born to a king and queen. (*God wanted us to know that Jesus was a human being, born to be the Savior of* all *people.*) Then, let them open the plain package. Ask, "In what ways does the small, plain package remind you of the birth of Jesus? (*It wasn't fancy.*)" If the students chose to open the plain package first, ask them what they think will be in the fancier package. Which package do they think most people would have chosen? Invite someone to open the fancier package. Then, use the discussion above that relates to the fancier package. Sing a Christmas song.

PRAYER "Lord, thank you for Christmas, when we celebrate the birth of Jesus. Thank you for sending Jesus to save us from our sins. Amen."

EPIPHANY I

TEXT   Psalm 96:10a

PREPARATION   Make or reuse the Epiphany banner mentioned in Opening 1. Make a large calendar, showing the months in the season of Epiphany (January and February, plus March, if Ash Wednesday falls in March). Write "Festival of the Epiphany of Our Lord" on January 6. Mark "Ash Wednesday." Choose an Epiphany song.

PRESENTATION

Review the symbols and the symbolism of the color on the Epiphany banner. Invite the students to share what they know about this season. Add this information. *Epiphany* means "a revealing, or showing" of something. During Epiphany, we celebrate those things that *show* us that Jesus is not just another man, but our Savior: the visit of the *Magi* (MAY-jy; sounds like *mayfly*), or Wise Men, and Jesus' baptism. Point to the first day of Epiphany on the calendar. Tell the students that January 6 is the day we celebrate the visit of the Magi. Ask, "What gifts did they bring Jesus? What does each gift tell us about Jesus? (*Gold symbolizes wealth and power. Jesus is our king. Frankincense was burned during Jewish worship. Jesus is God. Myrrh was used to prepare bodies for burial. Jesus died for our sins.*)" Ask, "When does Epiphany end?" Have someone point to the day before Ash Wednesday. If time allows, mention Mardi Gras and the traditions associated with it. Read the Bible text. Sing the song you chose.

PRAYER   "Lord, you sent the star to lead the Magi to Jesus. Send us to lead people to Jesus. Amen."

EPIPHANY II

TEXT   Matthew 2:1-12

PREPARATION   Several weeks in advance, decide on gifts the students could bring to help someone or an organization. Send letters home, suggesting what might be brought, when, and for whom. Invite a church school class or a mixed-age group of students to pantomime the Bible text as it is read. Make a large star to hang in front. Mary can hold a doll on her lap to represent Jesus. Write this prayer: "Lord, bless these gifts that we've brought. As the star led the Magi to Jesus, help us lead others to you. Amen."

PRESENTATION

Introduce the actors. Read the Bible text. After the skit, invite the students to place the gifts they brought near Jesus and Mary.

PRAYER   Point to the prayer. Say it together.

RELATED OPENING   23

EPIPHANY III

TEXT   Mark 1:9-11

PREPARATION   Cut a large dove from white paper. Tape it to the end of a yardstick or broom. Bring a shallow bowl. Write God's words from verse 11.

PRESENTATION _____

Invite the students to tell you the current church season. Remind them that Epiphany is the church season when we celebrate the different ways in which God showed us who Jesus is. Say, "Today we're going to dramatize the story of Jesus' baptism. Listen carefully to discover something important about Jesus." Choose three volunteers to be John, Jesus, and the dove. Explain that they will act out the story as you read it. Tell the rest that they will be God. Have them practice saying God's words from verse 11. Ask Jesus to kneel behind the bowl. Everyone will pretend there is water in the bowl.

Explain that Jesus was not baptized in a church or as a child, but as an adult in the Jordan River. Ask John to baptize Jesus by dipping his or her hand into the imaginary water and placing it on Jesus' head. Have the person with the dove stand behind Jesus, hiding it behind his or her back until it is time to hold it over Jesus' head. Tell the other students that you will point to them when it is time to say God's words. Read Mark 1:9-10. Signal the dove. Read the first half of verse 11, then point to the students and have them read God's words. Ask, "What did you learn about Jesus? *(Jesus is God's Son).*"

PRAYER   "God, thank you for the people who help us learn about Jesus. Help us share what we learn with others. Amen."

RELATED OPENINGS   23, 31, 39

ASH WEDNESDAY   13

TEXT   1 John 1:9

PREPARATION   Make or reuse the Lent banner mentioned in Opening 1. Make a large calendar showing the months in Lent. Write "Ash Wednesday" where it belongs. Choose an appropriate song. Write "Lent" on the chalkboard or chart paper.

PRESENTATION _____

Ask if someone remembers the name for the time of waiting that takes place before Christmas. *(Advent.)* Say, "There is another time of preparing and remembering in the church seasons. We call that time Lent." Bring out the banner. Say, "The first day of Lent is called Ash Wednesday, and we have a special worship service in the middle of the week." Share the following information about Ash Wednesday. In Old Testament times, before Jesus was born, the people asked God to forgive their sins by burning things on the altar at the temple. What is left in a fireplace or a campfire, when everything is burned up? *(Ashes.)* Sometimes the people who asked God for forgiveness would rub the ashes from the altar on their bodies to show how sorry they were that they had sinned. Do we still bring things to be burned on the altar so that God will forgive us?

(No.) Everything changed when God sent Jesus. In a few weeks we'll hear the stories of Jesus dying on the cross and God bringing him back to life on Easter. Because that happened, we know that God always forgives our sins. But on Ash Wednesday we stop and think about the things for which God has forgiven us. We tell God we are sorry for the things we have done and ask for God's help in living more like Jesus taught us. As a reminder that our sins are forgiven because of Jesus' death on the cross, some churches use ashes left from burned-up palm or olive branches. As people come to the front of the church, the pastor rubs a thumb in a bowl of ashes and draws a cross of ashes on the forehead of each person. Take your thumb and draw an invisible cross on your own forehead. Invite the children to do the same, as a reminder that their sins are forgiven.

PRAYER   Invite the students to pray silently, confessing their sins and thanking God for forgiveness.

RELATED OPENINGS   34, 37

LENT I

TEXT   Matthew 16:21

PREPARATION   Make or reuse the Lenten banner mentioned in Opening 1. Make a calendar as described in Opening 13. On the calendar, mark "Ash Wednesday" and the vernal equinox (March 21). Find out when the first full moon after the vernal equinox will appear. (Many commercial calendars show the phases of the moon.) Draw a circle on that date. Review the information included in Opening 13.

PRESENTATION

Draw the students' attention to the Lenten banner. Invite them to share the meanings of the symbols and the color purple. Say, "Jesus told his disciples what was going to happen to him. Listen to what he said." Read the Bible text. Discuss how Lent is a time to reflect on our spiritual life, confess our sins, and ask God's forgiveness. Show the students the calendar. Point to the first day of Lent. Invite them to share what they know about Ash Wednesday. Fill in with the information from Opening 13. Ask, "When does Lent end? (*The day before Easter.*) When is Easter? Is Easter always on the same date? What decides when Easter will be each year? (*It's always the first Sunday after the first full moon after the vernal equinox.*)" Using that formula, ask the students to figure out when Easter will be this year. Explain that Lent is 40 days long. Invite the students to count aloud the days of Lent as you point to each one. What do they notice? Tell them that the Sundays in Lent are not included. Count the number of Sundays. Subtract that number from their previous total and see if you get 40.

PRAYER   Lord, forgive our sins. Help us to grow closer to you during Lent. Amen.

LENT II

TEXT   2 Corinthians 5:15, 17

PREPARATION   Cover a bulletin board in your opening area with purple paper. At the top, place these words: "Lord, during Lent, help me to . . . " If a bulletin board is not available, make a display area using two sides of a large cardboard box. Bring 3" x 5" index cards, one per student; pencils, one per student; and tacks or pins. Invite adults or teens to help.

PRESENTATION

Read the Bible text. Say, "This verse talks about old things passing away. It says that in Christ everything becomes new. During Lent many people start new habits to help their faith grow." Ask the group to think of new habits they could start, such as setting aside a special prayer time; reading from their Bible, or a Bible storybook, every day; leading family devotions; or serving others in some way. Distribute the index cards and pencils. Invite the students to write a faith habit they would like to start on the card. After praying, fasten the cards to the bulletin board.

PRAYER   Ask the students to pray silently, finishing this phrase: "Lord, during Lent, help me to. . . " Complete the prayer by saying "amen."

SUGGESTED FOLLOW-UP   During subsequent weeks, invite the students to share their experiences with starting new habits.

HOLY WEEK I

TEXT John 12:12-13

PREPARATION Make or reuse the calendar described in Opening 14 and the Lent banner from Opening 1. Draw this crossword puzzle on a large sheet of paper. Write each clue (minus the answer) on a separate piece of paper. Fold and place them in a container.

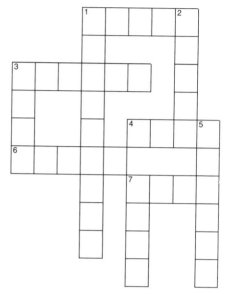

Across

1. He was paid 30 coins to turn Jesus over to the authorities. *(Judas.)*
3. The soldiers used these to make a crown for Jesus. *(Thorns.)*
4. Jesus surprised the disciples when he washed this part of their bodies. *(Feet.)*
6. During Jesus' last supper with his disciples, he called this "his body." *(Bread.)*
7. The people cut this kind of branch when they heard that Jesus was coming to Jerusalem. *(Palm.)*

Down

1. Jesus rode into this city on a donkey. *(Jerusalem.)*
2. This was rolled in front of the entrance to Jesus' tomb. *(Stone.)*
3. They put Jesus' body here after he died. *(Tomb.)*
5. Jesus went to this building to teach people about God. *(Temple.)*
7. After eating his last meal, Jesus went to the garden to do this. *(Pray.)*

PRESENTATION

Read the Bible text. Say, "Every year the Christian church celebrates this event. What do we call this day? *(Palm Sunday.)*" Write "Palm Sunday" on the appropriate space on the calendar. Explain that Palm Sunday marks the beginning of Holy Week. Call attention to the crossword puzzle. Explain that it will help them remember some of the events of Holy Week. Do the crossword puzzle, having volunteers choose the clues and write the answers in the appropriate spaces on the puzzle. Help with spelling. Put aside clues to which they don't know the answer, and return to them at the end. Once the puzzle is done, point to the Thursday of Holy Week. Say, "On this day we remember Jesus' last supper with his disciples. What do we call this day? *(Holy Thursday, or Maundy Thursday.)*" Write whichever term you prefer on the space for that day. Point to Friday and say, "On this day, we remember that Jesus died on a cross so that our sins would be forgiven. What do we call this day? *(Good Friday.)*" Label it on the calendar. Point to the banner. Invite the students to tell which symbols stand for events we remember during Holy Week.

PRAYER Lord, we praise you for being our king. We thank you for dying so that our sins would be forgiven. Amen.

RELATED OPENINGS 34, 38

HOLY WEEK II

TEXT 1 John 2:1-2

PREPARATION Bring pictures or objects to represent each of these symbols: palm branches (Luke 19:29-38), king's crown (Luke 19:29-38), bag with coins (Luke 22:1-6), basin of water (John 13:3-15), cup with grape juice and unleavened bread (Luke 22:7-8, 14-20), cup and cross (Luke 22:39-46), rooster (Luke 22:54-62), purple robe and crown of thorns (Mark 15:16-20), large brown paper cross (Mark 15:21-25), and a white cloth (Mark 15:42-47). Familiarize yourself with the Bible verses accompanying each of the objects so that you can help the students remember the story associated with each object. These verses will not be read during the presentation. Set the objects on a table in the same order as they are listed. Leave room for the cross. Place the cross on a table near the entrance. Put markers and crayons with it.

PRESENTATION

Have each student write his or her name on the cross. Call attention to the objects on the table. Say, "These objects will help us remember some of the important events that took place during the week before Jesus died." Hold up the palm branches. Invite someone to tell what palm branches had to do with Jesus' last week. Continue, in the same way, with each of the other objects, adding information as needed. When you reach the cross, ask volunteers to carry it up to the table. Ask, "What happened on the cross? Why did Jesus die? *(Jesus died for our sins.)*" Hold up the white cloth and ask, "What happened soon after Jesus died? *(His body was wrapped in a linen cloth and laid in a tomb. A large stone was rolled in front of the entrance.)* On Easter, we'll talk about what happened next."

PRAYER Invite the students to compose a prayer. Say it together.

RELATED OPENINGS 34, 38

EASTER I

18

TEXT Luke 23:55—24:7

PREPARATION Make or reuse the Easter banner described in Opening 1. Make butterfly wings from white paper, proportional to the cross in Opening 17. Decide how to fasten the wings to the cross to form a butterfly. Place each wing on a separate table along with markers or crayons. Make a large calendar, including all the months in the Easter season. Mark "Good Friday" and the "Festival of Pentecost" on it. Write "RESURRECTION" on the chalkboard or chart paper.

PRESENTATION

As the students arrive, invite them to write their names with bright colors on one of the wings. Gather the students and read the Bible text. Ask, "What good news did the women hear? What is the good news we tell others at Easter? *(He is risen!)* What is the big word we use to describe Jesus' coming back to life?" Point to "RESURRECTION." Say, "On Easter we celebrate the resurrection." Call attention to the Easter banner. Discuss how each symbol represents the resurrection. Invite some students to bring up the butterfly wings so you can attach them to the cross. If you used Opening 17, say, "We wrote our names on this cross to show that Jesus died for the sins of each of us. Why do you think we wrote our names on the butterfly wings?" Help them understand that because Jesus rose from the dead, those who believe in Jesus as their Savior have no reason to fear dying, as they will live forever with God in heaven. Divide the students into sections. Have the first section chant, "He is risen!" Invite the second section to join them. Add sections until everyone is chanting. On a predetermined signal, everyone should shout, "He is risen indeed!"

PRAYER "We praise you, Lord, for the resurrection and the gift of eternal life. Amen."

RELATED OPENING 35

EASTER II

TEXT Mark 15:46—16:7

PREPARATION Bring a pot of blooming plants that grow from bulbs. On a paper sack, write in large letters: *(NAME OF FLOWER) BULBS*. Before the students arrive, place the plant in the bag and staple the top shut. Set the bag on a front table. Cut one small square of paper per student. On a table near the entrance, place the paper squares, pencils, and a container.

PRESENTATION

As the students enter, have them write their name on a paper square and place it in the container. Hold up the bag. Ask, "What's in this bag?" Invite someone to describe a bulb. Say, "Today one of you is going to win this bag of bulbs." Choose a name from the container. Invite that person to look in the bag. Ask, "What did you expect to find? Are you surprised?" Help them show the other students the flowers. Request that they leave them on the table for all to enjoy until the opening is over. Then say, "*(Name of student)* had a surprise. The Bible story I'm going to read is about a surprise." Read Mark 15:46-47 and Mark 16:1-2. Ask, "Who, or what, did the women expect to find in the tomb?" Then, read Mark 16:3-7. Ask, "What was their surprise?"

PRAYER Invite the students to shout "He is risen!" whenever you pause in the following prayer: "Lord, thank you for the messenger who told the women the good news *(pause)*. Thank you for the women who told the disciples *(pause)*. Thank you for the people who have told us *(pause)*. Help us to tell everyone that Jesus is not dead, *(pause)*. Amen."

RELATED OPENING 45

PENTECOST I

TEXT Joel 2:28

PREPARATION Make or reuse the Pentecost banner mentioned in Opening 1. Make a large calendar that includes the months necessary to show Passover, Easter, and the Festival of Pentecost. Mark those three days on the calendar. Write the names of the other complete months included in the Pentecost season on a separate sheet of paper. Make a large calendar showing the month when Pentecost ends. Mark the first Sunday in Advent on it. Write "Pentecost," "The Feast of Weeks," "Shavuoth" on another sheet of paper. Write this prayer on a large sheet of paper: "Lord, thank you for Pentecost, when we celebrate the gift of the Holy Spirit. Fill us with your Spirit. Help our faith grow. Help the Christian church grow, too. Amen."

PRESENTATION

Point to the Pentecost banner. Invite the students to share what they know about Pentecost. Share the following information. Pentecost is the Greek name for the Israelite festival called Shavuoth, the Feast of Weeks, celebrating the wheat harvest. Point to the list of names for Pentecost. Pentecost means "50th." The Greeks named it that because Pentecost came 50 days after Passover. Invite the students to count the number of days between Passover and Pentecost. The Pentecost season lasts until Advent. Christians celebrate Pentecost because that is the day when the Holy Spirit came and gave the apostles the ability to tell others about Jesus. Some Old Testament prophets had promised that God would send the Spirit. Read the Bible text. The Christian church celebrates its birthday on the first day of Pentecost.

Look at the symbols on the banner. Which ones stand for the Holy Spirit? Which ones stand for the Christian church? Review the symbolism of red and green.

PRAYER   Read the prayer in unison.

RELATED OPENINGS   36, 39

PENTECOST II _____ 21

TEXT   Acts 2:1-17, 32-38, 41-42

PREPARATION   Several weeks in advance, arrange for one of the older classes and that class's teacher to prepare the Bible text as a skit. Bring a basin and a small pebble. Fill the basin with water. Place it on the floor, or on a low table in front of the students.

PRESENTATION _____

Introduce the skit. After it has been performed, invite the students to make comments or ask questions. The students may have questions about the apostles' ability to speak in languages they never studied. Explain that during Shavuoth (the Feast of Weeks, or Pentecost), Jewish people from many places came to Jerusalem. When the Spirit gave the apostles the ability to speak in other languages, they were able to tell each person in his or her own language about Jesus. These people returned to their countries and told others about Jesus.

PRAYER   Hold the pebble over the water and ask, "What will happen if I drop this pebble?" After hearing the students' ideas, invite them to gather around the basin. Drop the pebble. Call their attention to the spreading ripples. Say, "Before the Holy Spirit came, Jesus had a few followers. Then the Spirit came. In one day, over 3000 people decided to follow Jesus. Each of us can be like a pebble. When we tell someone about Jesus, the news spreads like ripples on water." Invite the students to pray silently, asking God to help them tell others about Jesus.

RELATED OPENINGS   23, 39, 92

RALLY DAY _____ 22

TEXT   Luke 10:20b

PREPARATION   Bring markers. Invite the teachers to meet with you before the opening. Explain the rules for "Teacher Jump Up" to them. Write "Our names are. . . " at the top of a large sheet of paper. Place a row of chairs, one per teacher, facing the area where the students will be sitting.

PRESENTATION _____

Invite each person to write his or her first name on the "Our names are. . . " list. If their first name is the same as another child's, and it is already there, have them draw a smiling face after it. Introduce yourself and welcome everyone. Read the Bible text. Say, "Names are important. They're so important that they're written in heaven. They're also written on this list." Point to the "Our names are. . . " list. Say, "Stand when you hear me call your name."

Read the list. Invite the teachers to sit in the row of chairs. Ask them to stand as they are being introduced. After each introduction, have the students repeat the name. Then, play "Teacher Jump Up." The first teacher jumps up and the students call out his or her name. Then the second teacher jumps up. After the students have called out that teacher's name, the first teacher pops up and is named. The third teacher jumps up, followed by the second; and then, the first. Each time a teacher jumps up the students say his or her name. Continue in the same way through the entire group of teachers. If there are many teachers, only the three previous ones should jump up to be named.

PRAYER "Lord, you know each of us by name. Help us learn each other's names and get to know each other better. Amen."

CELEBRATING FRIENDSHIP 23

TEXT Proverbs 17:17a

PREPARATION Several weeks in advance, encourage the students to invite friends to come to church with them for this special celebration. Ask each person to bring a small piece of fresh fruit, if possible. Send a note home explaining what will be happening. Bring name tags and markers. Have a large mixing spoon, a large bowl, and one or more paring knives. Arrange for several adults to cut up the fruit. Place a table at the front of the room. Provide small paper plates, toothpicks, and napkins for the students. Write and display the Bible text.

PRESENTATION

Welcome the students and their friends. Draw their attention to the pile of fruit on the table. Compare the differences in people to the differences in fruits. Ask the adults to take the fruit, wash it, cut it into bite-size pieces, and mix it in the bowl. While the fruit is being prepared, divide the students and their friends into groups of four to eight. You need at least three groups. Point to the Bible text. Ask each group to make up a different rhythmic way to say it. Encourage them to put motions with the words. After they've finished creating and practicing, ask each group to demonstrate their rhythmic verse. Say, "Each group created a slightly different rhythm. God created each of us to be different from everyone else. Life is more interesting because we're different." Distribute plates, toothpicks, and napkins. Discuss the result of mixing the fruits. During the discussion, have your helpers ladle the fruit onto the students' plates. Ask them to pause for a prayer before eating. Pray the prayer printed below. While eating, encourage people to share good experiences they've had with friends.

PRAYER "Lord, thank you for this friendship fruit salad. As we eat it, help us remember that we can be friends with all different kinds of people. Help us show love to our friends. Amen."

RELATED OPENING 42

CELEBRATING OUR CHURCH 24

TEXT Psalm 122:1

PREPARATION Find members of your church who have slides, photographs, or stories about the history of your church that they could share with the students. Write and display the Bible text.

Invite the students to read the Bible text in unison. Say, "Today we're going to celebrate the anniversary of our church. Our church is *(number of years)* years old today. *(Names of guests)* have come to tell us about the history of our church." After the presentations, thank your guests for sharing.

PRAYER "Lord, thank you for sending *(names of guests)* to tell us about our church. Thank you for the people who started our church. Thank you for making us part of this church. Amen."

RELATED OPENING 33

CREATION CELEBRATION _____ 25

TEXT Psalm 148

PREPARATION Several weeks before this opening, ask one or more classes to illustrate people, animals, or natural objects that praise the Lord in Psalm 148. Arrange for an older class to read the psalm. They can read it in unison, or divide it into parts to be read by individuals, or small groups.

PRESENTATION _____

Say, "Today we're going to celebrate God's creation. I'm thinking of something God created." Invite the students to ask yes or no questions to discover the item. After it has been guessed, say a short prayer, thanking God for that item. The person who guessed correctly thinks of the next item. Pray after each item is guessed. Continue by inviting those who drew the pictures to stand in a line in front. Introduce the psalm readers. After they have read, ask the artists and the audience to point out things they heard named in the psalm. Collect the drawings and use them to create a "Praise the Lord" bulletin board display.

PRAYER (Included in the presentation.)

RELATED OPENING 48

WORLD DAY _____ 26

TEXT 1 John 3:11

PREPARATION Choose four or more countries from different areas of the world. Set up centers, representing each country. Have one short activity at each center. Some ideas: tasting a food, learning how to say a phrase, learning a dance, playing an instrument, learning to use a toy or implement, or looking at photographs. If possible, invite people who have lived in that country, or visited it, to be at each center. Invite adults or teens to be center teachers and helpers. Plan an area where simple religious songs from other countries will be sung.

Invite the students to visit the centers. After they have had time to visit each center, gather everyone together to sing the songs from other countries. Read the Bible text.

PRAYER "Thank you, Lord, for the world in which we live. Thank you for all the different people who share it with us. Help us to love one another. Amen."

RELATED OPENINGS 90, 92

CELEBRATING CHILDREN 27

TEXT Mark 10:13-16

PREPARATION Bring a plant that was started from a seed and a seed of that plant. Choose a song appropriate to this topic.

PRESENTATION

Show the plant and the seed. Ask, "Which is more important?" After the students have voiced their opinions, help them realize that neither is more important than the other. They are both important. There would not be one without the other. Ask, "Who is more important, an adult or a child?" After some discussion, say, "There is a story in the Bible that will help us discover Jesus' answer to this question." Read Mark 10:13. Ask, "What happened next? What did Jesus say?" Read verses 14 through 16, and compare them with the students' responses to the above questions. Emphasize that Jesus loves both adults and children. Sing the song you chose.

PRAYER "Lord, thank you for children. Help these children who love you to grow into adults who love you. Amen."

RELATED OPENINGS 65, 73

ALL SAINTS' DAY 28

TEXT Ephesians 5:1

PREPARATION Provide name tags and markers. On each name tag, write "Saint _____."
Choose a song about saints. Write this prayer on a large sheet of paper.
Group 1: Lord, thank you for all the faithful people who have lived before us.
All: Help us be like them.
Group 2: Thank you for faithful people today.
All: Help us be like them.
Group 3: Thank you for being our Lord.
All: Help us be like you. Amen.

PRESENTATION

Request that each student write his or her name in the blank space on a name tag. Invite the students to imitate your actions. Then, do an action. Do another. Then, sit quietly. Once everyone has settled down, say, "Today we're celebrating All Saints' Day. Saints are followers of Jesus, people who try to imitate God." Read the Bible text. Ask, "What does it mean to imitate, or try to be like God? What is God like?"

Write a list of God's characteristics. Include loving, caring, merciful, forgiving, and faithful. As a group, define each term so that everyone is able to understand what it means. Say, "On All Saints' Day, Christians praise and thank God for all the saints who have lived and are living. We thank God that we have been called to be saints." Sing the song you chose.

PRAYER   Divide the students into three groups. Assign each group a portion of the prayer. Read it responsively.

RELATED OPENINGS 62–76

PASSOVER 29

TEXT Exodus 12:1-14

PREPARATION Bring a current calendar that has *Passover* marked on it.

PRESENTATION

Ask a volunteer to point to Passover on the calendar. Mention that it is a major Jewish festival that is celebrated every year and has been for thousands of years. The last supper that Jesus ate with his disciples was a special Passover meal. Say, "Today we're going to learn about the first Passover. A long time ago the Israelites moved to Egypt because there was not enough food in their land. Pharaoh, the leader of Egypt, gave them a good piece of land on which to live. Many years went by. Other pharaohs came to power. They turned the Israelites into their slaves. The Israelites were forced to build Pharaoh's cities and pyramids. They had to work hard. Many were whipped and beaten. The Israelites prayed that God would save them. God chose a man named Moses to lead the Israelites out of Egypt. Moses went to Pharaoh and said, 'Let my people go.' Pharaoh replied, 'No!' God decided to show Pharaoh his great power, but Pharaoh was very stubborn. Each time I say, 'Pharaoh said . . . ' everyone say, 'NO!' God turned the Egyptians' water into blood, but Pharaoh said . . . (NO!). God covered Egypt with frogs, but Pharaoh said . . . (NO!). God changed the dust into gnats, but Pharaoh said . . . (NO!). God sent flies to cover the ground, but

Pharaoh said . . . (NO!). God gave the Egyptians' animals a terrible disease, but Pharaoh said . . . (NO!). God made boils, or sores, appear on the Egyptians and their animals, but Pharaoh said . . . (NO!). God sent hail to Egypt, but Pharaoh said . . . (NO!). God sent locusts to eat the Egyptians' crops, but Pharaoh said . . . (NO!). God covered Egypt with darkness for three days, but Pharaoh said . . . (NO!). Nine times terrible things happened to the Egyptians. Nine times Moses said, 'LET MY PEOPLE GO.' Nine times Pharaoh replied, 'NO!' Then God told Moses that he would punish the Egyptians one last time. This time the Egyptians would be convinced to let the Israelites go. God told Moses that the angel of death was coming, and every firstborn son of the Egyptians and the firstborn of their cattle would die. God gave Moses special instructions. If the Israelites obeyed God's instructions, they would be safe. Their sons and their cattle would not be harmed." Read the Bible text. Have the students listen for God's instructions. List them. Say, "The Israelites obeyed. This time Pharaoh let them go. Every year Jewish people around the world celebrate Passover. They remember how God led them out of slavery to freedom."

PRAYER   "Lord, you sent Moses to free the Israelites from slavery in Egypt. You sent Jesus to free us from slavery to sin. Thank you for loving us so much. Amen."

RELATED OPENINGS   17, 20, 38, 40, 53

SUGGESTED FOLLOW-UP   Invite a person of the Jewish faith to share how they celebrate Passover.

OPENINGS SUITABLE FOR OTHER CELEBRATIONS
Valentine's Day: 23
Love: 42, 97, 98
Earth Day: 25
Labor Day: 57
Reformation Sunday: 63
Thanksgiving: 48

ANGELS 30

TEXTS   Exodus 33:2a; Psalm 91:11; Matthew 28:1-3; Luke 1:26-33; 2:8-14; 22:39-43; Hebrews 1:14

PREPARATION   Choose two songs that mention angels.

PRESENTATION

Lead the students in singing the songs. Ask, "What kind of beings do these songs mention?" Invite the students to share their ideas about angels. Say, "Today we are going to find out what the Bible says about angels." After reading each Bible text, ask the students what they learned about angels. Make a list.

PRAYER   Pray, using the list. For example, if "Angels protect us" is on the list, you could thank God for their protection.

BAPTISM 31

TEXT   Acts 2:38

PREPARATION   Draw a shell with three drops of water. Invite your pastor to speak to the students about Baptism or give you suggestions for discussing Baptism. If possible, meet where baptisms take place in your church.

PRESENTATION

Display the shell drawing. Say, "This symbol stands for something we do in our church. What might that be?" Give clues if necessary. Once someone says, "Baptism," invite the students to tell you what they know about Baptism. Read the Bible text. Ask, "What does this verse tell us about Baptism?" Invite the students to listen and ask questions as you or the pastor tells about Baptism in your church.

PRAYER   "Dear Lord, thank you for Baptism. Thank you for forgiving our sins and giving us the gift of the Holy Spirit. Amen."

RELATED OPENINGS   12, 37, 39, 49

CHRISTIAN

TEXT   Acts 11:26b

PREPARATION   Contact three students to see if they would be
willing to come dressed in the uniform of an
organization to which they belong, such as Girl
Scouts, a band, or an athletic team. Draw a fish
symbol like the one at the beginning of this
opening. Hang it near the entrance. Choose an
appropriate song.

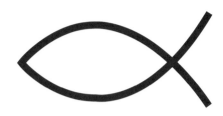

PRESENTATION

Have the uniformed volunteers come forward. Invite
the students to guess to which organization each
volunteer belongs. Have them explain how they
could tell. Summarize by saying, "In each case you
could tell by what they were wearing. How can you
tell if someone is a Christian?" Help the students
realize that you can't recognize a Christian by what
he or she wears. Say, "In the early days of the
Christian church, Christians were killed or thrown
into prison because the government did not trust
them. Christians had to be very careful so that the
wrong people didn't find out they believed in Jesus.
But Christians thought of a secret way to find out
who else was Christian. When they met someone,
they would trace a semicircle with a stick in the
dirt." Draw a semicircle. Continue, "If the other
person drew another semicircle, so that the two
formed a fish shape, then the first person knew that
the second person was a Christian. The fish was
their secret symbol. They marked this symbol on
their places of worship, too." Ask the students to
raise their hand if they've ever seen a fish symbol
that looks like the one you drew. Ask how many of
them are wearing a fish symbol. Say, "What is a
common symbol that Christians sometimes wear
today? (*A cross.*) Being a Christian is more than just
wearing a cross. Some people wear crosses just as a
piece of jewelry or a decoration. How can someone
really tell you're a Christian?" Discuss the kinds of
behavior that might indicate that someone is a
Christian. Be sure to include loving and forgiving.
Sing the song.

PRAYER   "Lord, may our actions show others that we are Christians. Amen."

RELATED OPENINGS   37, 42, 90–101

CHURCH

TEXT   Ephesians 1:23a; 4:16

PREPARATION   Make simple drawings of eyes, mouth, hands, and feet on four sheets of paper. Bring
a drinking glass. Write each of the following prayer lines on a separate strip of paper:
(1) Lord, thank you for the different people in our church. (2) Thank you for the
different things each of us can do. (3) Show us how each of us can work in our
church. Write the following prayer on the chalkboard or chart paper: "Help us work
together. Help us grow. Amen." Put a glass of fresh water on a table at the front of the
room.

PRESENTATION

Show the students the glass of water and give the
four drawings to volunteers. Say, "What would each
of these parts of your body have to do in order for
you to come up here and drink this water?" Ask the
remaining students to vote, by show of hands, on
which part would act first, second, third, and fourth.

Either "feet" or "eyes" could be first, followed by "hands" and "mouth." Suggest that the "eyes" point to the glass as if seeing it, and the "feet" walk to it. Ask the "hands" and "mouth" to follow the "feet" or "eyes" to the glass. Have the "hands" pick it up and give the "mouth" a drink. Once the water has been drunk, say, "We just watched different parts of the body work together to get a job done. In the Bible, the church is compared to a body. Listen as I read these verses to see what you learn about the church." After reading, ask the group to tell what they learned.

PRAYER Choose three volunteers and give each a numbered prayer strip. Show the other students the prayer that everyone will read after the third student has finished.

RELATED OPENINGS 90–101

CROSS

34

TEXT Mark 8:34

PREPARATION Find these four types of crosses illustrated in Appendix A at the back of this book: anchor cross, Latin cross, cross crosslet, and the cross in glory. Draw a large outline of each cross on a separate piece of 9" x 12" construction paper. Use a different color paper for each cross. Cut out the cross, then cut each one in half or in fourths, depending on the number needed for the group. If more than 16 pieces are desired, make multiples of some of the crosses. Fasten one or more sheets of chart paper to a wall or a chalkboard. Provide several glue sticks. Choose a song about following Jesus.

PRESENTATION

Mix the puzzle pieces and give each child a puzzle piece as he or she enters. When all pieces have been distributed, ask the students to stand up and move around the room and find those who have the remaining pieces needed to complete a cross. Ask each pair or group to come forward and glue their pieces together on the chart paper. Thank them for their participation. Point out the Latin cross, which is the style usually associated with Christ's death. Ask the children what happened on the cross. (*Jesus died.*) Ask, "If such a terrible thing happened on a cross, why do we have them in our churches and why do people wear them as jewelry?" (*Because Jesus rose from the dead on Easter and lives today.*) Explain,

"The cross is important to Christians because it reminds us of God's love and of Jesus' power to save us." The anchor cross represents hope. Jesus is like an anchor that holds a boat securely in one spot so that it doesn't drift away. The cross crosslet represents the four directions of the compass, where the good news of Jesus was spread. The sunrise on the cross of glory represents the new day of salvation that dawned when Jesus rose from the dead, and the circle indicates eternity. Read the Bible text. When Jesus asks us to carry our cross, it means to live in the way he taught us, being loving, caring, and forgiving. Sing the song you chose.

PRAYER "Lord, thank you for reminding us, through the cross, of how much you love us. May the cross encourage us to be your followers. Amen."

RELATED OPENINGS 13, 16, 17, 37, 40

SUGGESTED FOLLOW-UP Tour your church and take note of the different styles of crosses found there.

ETERNAL LIFE

35

TEXT   John 3:16

PREPARATION   At least a week in advance, arrange for another adult to be present during this opening and lead the students in singing a song of his or her choice. Bring cookies or crackers, one for each child, and store them somewhere outside the opening area.

PRESENTATION

Greet the students and introduce the other adult who is present. Tell the group, "I am going to leave the room for a few minutes. While I'm gone, *(name of guest)* will sing a song with you. When I come back, I will have something special for each of you." Leave the room and return a few minutes later with the cookies. As you distribute them, ask, "Did you believe me when I said I would be back and bring something for you?" (Get responses.) "When Jesus came back to life on Easter, after dying on the cross, he brought the very best gift in the world for each of us." Read the Bible text. Continue, "Did anyone hear what that gift is? It is eternal life. *Eternal* means 'forever.' Does that mean that we will never die? No, but it does mean that we don't need to worry about what will happen to us or to those we love when we die. God has promised to be with us all the time here on earth, and when we die we will live with God in heaven forever. We don't know where heaven is or exactly what it is like, but we can be sure that it is a place where we are safe and happy and loved. What a wonderful gift!"

PRAYER "Thank you, God, for sending Jesus to show how much you loved your people. Thank you for the gift of eternal life. Amen."

RELATED OPENINGS 18, 45

SUGGESTED FOLLOW-UP Ask the students to draw their impressions of what heaven looks like. Display the drawings and descriptions of them, if needed, for others in the church to see.

FAITH

36

TEXT   Hebrews 11:1

PREPARATION   Place on a tray some bite-size pieces of food that students would consider delicious and some that they would rather not eat. Bring three blindfolds. Choose a song about faith. Write this prayer: "Lord, give us faith to know that you love and care for us. Help our faith grow. Amen."

PRESENTATION

Invite three volunteers to come up. Ask each to say which food on the tray they like best and which they like least. Write down their choices. Blindfold the volunteers. Say, "We're going to do an experiment to see how much faith you have in me. I'm going to give each of you a bite of the food that you said you like best. You're blindfolded, so you won't be able to see what I'm doing. Do you have faith that I'll do what I say?" If someone is doubtful, ask why. Say, "Wouldn't it be a good joke if I gave you the food you like least?" Wait for a reaction. "But I'm not going to do that. You can trust me." Ask them to open their mouths. Give each a taste of the food they said they'd like best. Remove the blindfolds.

Thank them for helping. Read the Bible text. Assure the students that even though they can't always have faith in people, they can always have faith in God. Sing the song about faith.

PRAYER   Pray the prayer together.

FORGIVENESS 37

TEXTS   Ephesians 1:7a, 4:32; 1 John 1:9; Matthew 18:21-22

PREPARATION   Bring a basin, pitcher of water, dish soap, dish cloth, dish towel, and two opaque mugs. Dirty the outside of one mug. Dirty the inside of the other.

PRESENTATION

Hold up the mugs so that the students can only see the outsides. Ask, "From which mug would you rather drink?" After they've responded, tip the mugs so the students can see the insides. Ask, "Which one would you rather drink out of now? What do these mugs need?" When the students mention washing, squirt some dish soap in the basin, fill it with water, and begin washing the mugs. As you wash them, say, "When we sin, we're like these mugs. Sometimes people know about our sin. (Invite examples.) Then we're like the mug that was dirty on the outside. Sometimes no one but God knows about our sin. (Invite other examples.) Then we're like the mug that was dirty on the inside. Either

way, we need to get rid of our sin. I used soap and water to get rid of the dirt. How do we get rid of sin?" When someone mentions forgiveness, ask, "What does the Bible teach us about forgiveness?" List the things they mention. If they miss one of these ideas, read the accompanying Bible text and ask the students what it means. Add it to the list. (1) In Christ's death and resurrection our sins are forgiven (Ephesians 1:7a). (2) We forgive each other just as God forgives us (Ephesians 4:32). (3) If we confess our sins, God will forgive us (1 John 1:9). (4) There is no limit to the number of times we forgive someone (Matthew 18:21-22).

PRAYER   Say the Lord's Prayer together. Listen for the part that mentions forgiveness.

HOLY COMMUNION 38

TEXT   Matthew 26:26-28

PREPARATION   Gather the different items used by your congregation in the preparation and celebration of Holy Communion. Display them on a table. You may want to invite your pastor to come and answer questions about your congregation's practices. Choose a prayer used by your church during Holy Communion.

PRESENTATION

Ask the students if they ever have special meals at home to celebrate a special event. (*Answers may include birthdays, Christmas, Thanksgiving, Easter.*) On these occasions, are any special things put on the table—perhaps special dishes or a tablecloth? Point to the items on the table and invite the students to guess for what special occasion these things are

used. (*Holy Communion, the Lord's Supper, Eucharist.*) Introduce these names and emphasize the one used most commonly in your congregation. Hold up each item and discuss what it is and how the students have seen it used. Explain, "This is a special meal we come to with other people who believe in Jesus Christ." Read the Bible text, then say, "We believe that Jesus comes to us in the bread and wine (or grape juice). Holy Communion reminds us that Jesus is still with us, inviting us to a special meal, like he did with the disciples at the Last Supper." Ask, "What do we celebrate in Holy Communion?" Give the students time to respond. Say, "We celebrate the forgiveness of our sins. We all know that we have sinned, but we also know that God has forgiven our sins through Jesus' death. So we celebrate God's great love for us by sharing this meal together."

PRAYER   Say the prayer you chose.

RELATED OPENINGS   17, 37

HOLY SPIRIT 39

TEXT   Acts 1:8

PREPARATION   Bring a few items that need moving air in order to work: pinwheel, whistle, wind instrument, wind chimes, mobile, or kite. Bring a few items that need to be filled with air in order to work: balloon, bicycle tire, inner tube, air mattress, swimming pool toys, or basketball. Keep these items in a box. Place a table in front.

PRESENTATION

Pull one item at a time from the box. Ask the students to tell you what it is and how to use it. Invite volunteers to show how each item works. Help the students realize that each of these items needs power—in this case, the power of air—to do its job. Say, "Before Jesus rose to heaven, he told his disciples to wait for a power that would help them spread the good news to the ends of the earth. The disciples waited. Then, one day a mighty wind filled the room in which they were meeting. The wind was God's Spirit. To show that these people were being given God's power, the Holy Spirit, God made a flame of fire appear above their heads. The power of the Holy Spirit made it possible for the disciples to speak many different languages, so that people all over would learn about Jesus."

PRAYER   "God, fill us with your spirit, so we can tell everyone about Jesus. Amen."

RELATED OPENINGS   12, 21, 49, 92

LAMB OF GOD 40

TEXT   John 1:29

PREPARATION   Bring in pictures, or stuffed animals, to represent six different real animals. Have at least one predator, one large animal, and a lamb. Display the animals on a front table. Draw an enlarged version of the lamb symbol that appears in Appendix A at the back of this book. Keep it hidden.

PRESENTATION

Ask the students to identify each animal. Say, "If you were to compare Jesus to one of these animals, which one would it be?" After each response, ask the student to tell how Jesus is like the animal they chose. Say, "John the Baptist compared Jesus to one of these animals. Let's find out which one it was."

Read the Bible text. Explain that in Old Testament times, God required the people to sacrifice animals as a sign that they were sorry for their sins. Lambs were one of the animals that were sacrificed. Say, "Who sacrificed himself for our sins?" Discuss how Jesus took the place of the lamb. Because Jesus died for all our sins, we no longer need to sacrifice animals. (If you've done Opening 29, compare Jesus' sacrifice to the Passover lamb.) Hold up the lamb symbol. Say, "Many Christian artists draw a lamb similar to this one to symbolize Jesus, the Lamb of God, the one who saves us from our sins." Encourage them to look for this symbol in other places.

PRAYER "Thank you, God, for sending Jesus to die for our sins. Amen."

RELATED OPENINGS 34, 37, 42

THE LORD'S PRAYER 41

TEXT Matthew 6:9-13

PREPARATION Write the Lord's Prayer as it is prayed in your church. Think of possible actions that could be used with the Lord's Prayer. Arrange for someone to bring a video camera and tape the students doing their motions. Set up a VCR and TV in front.

PRESENTATION

Read the Bible text. Say, "These are the words that Jesus taught his disciples to pray. What do we call this prayer? When we say the Lord's Prayer in our church, what words do we use?" Invite the students to say the Lord's Prayer. Point to the words for those students who may not know this prayer. Say, "Sometimes when we say a memorized prayer, we don't think about the meaning of the words. But today we're going to put actions with the words to help us understand it better." Go through the prayer phrase by phrase, briefly discussing what each means and what action would help people understand the meaning. As each action is chosen, videotape the students saying that phrase and doing the action.

PRAYER Rewind the tape. Place it in the VCR. Invite the students to say the Lord's Prayer and do the motions along with the tape. Then, try to do it without the tape.

SUGGESTED FOLLOW-UP Do the Lord's Prayer with motions during subsequent openings. Teach this version of the Lord's Prayer to your congregation.

LOVE 42

TEXT Mark 12:30-31

PREPARATION Cut a large heart from red paper. On it write "love" in several languages, excluding English. Some possibilities are: *amor*, Spanish; *liebe*, German; *hlub* (hloo), Hmong; uthando (oo-TAN-doe), Zulu; *amour*, French. If someone in your congregation speaks another language, ask them to tell you their word for "love" and write it on the heart. Learn to sign "love" in American Sign Language: close hands into fists and cross wrists over the chest. Choose some appropriate songs.

PRESENTATION

Point to the heart. Ask, "What do you think of when you see a heart?" Point to the words in the heart. Help the students pronounce them. Ask, "What English word is represented by these words?" When they guess, write "love" in the heart. Teach the sign for "love." Say, "I wrote 'love' in all these languages to remind us that God loves everyone. Who does God want us to love?" After the students have expressed their ideas, read the Bible text. Ask, "Whom should we love? (*God, ourselves, our neighbors.*)" Talk about how much we're to love God, ourselves, and our neighbors. Say, "When we love God first, God gives us the ability to love ourselves and our neighbors." Sing the songs you chose.

PRAYER Invite the students to close their eyes and pray silently, telling God of their love. After a minute, ask them to pray, asking God to help them love themselves. Then, invite them to ask God to help them love their neighbors. Close by praying, "Lord, thank you for your gift of love, which is much greater than any love we can ever give. Thank you for loving us. Thank you for loving everyone. Amen."

RELATED OPENINGS 90, 98

PEACE 43

TEXT	John 14:27
PREPARATION	Think of a time when you were in a scary situation, but you felt God's peace. Choose a song about peace.

PRESENTATION

Read the Bible text. Discuss what it means. Say, "God is always with us, even in scary situations. Sometimes we're so busy being scared that we forget that God is with us. When we remember God, then God's peace can fill us." Share your experience. Encourage the students to ask questions and share their experiences. Sing the song.

PRAYER Invite the students to say "Give us your peace" each time you pause in this prayer: "Lord, when we're feeling sad, (*pause*). When we're feeling alone, (*pause*). When we're scared, (*pause*). When we're troubled, (*pause*). Thank you for always being with us. Amen."

RELATED OPENINGS 74, 75

PRAYER 44

TEXT	Romans 1:9b
PREPARATION	Bring a bulletin board or a scrapbook and sticky notes or colorful pieces of paper. On the bulletin board, write the words of the Bible text. Set the paper, writing tools, and any tape or pins that are needed near the bulletin board. Think of a personal prayer request that you could share. Choose a song about praying.

PRESENTATION

Discuss some of the following questions: What is prayer? Why do we pray? What do you pray about? Emphasize that prayer is the way we communicate with God. While praying, we can praise and thank God. We can ask God to give us guidance or things we need. We can pray for the needs of others, or we can sit quietly and listen to God. Call attention to the bulletin board. Invite the students to read the Bible text aloud. Say, "It's important for Christians to pray for others. We're going to use this board to let others know what we would like them to pray about. For example, I'd appreciate it if you would pray. . ." Share your prayer request. Demonstrate how to place a request on the board. Show them where the board will be placed. Encourage them to check the board each week and pray for the requests. Invite the students to sing the song several times while those who would like to make prayer requests write and post them. Ask older students to assist younger students.

PRAYER   Pray, incorporating the requests.

RELATED OPENING   66

SUGGESTED FOLLOW-UP   Refer to the prayer board in subsequent weeks and pray for the requests.

RESURRECTION   45

TEXT   John 11:25-26

PREPARATION   Gather at least one of these pairs of items, or pictures of them: chrysalis and butterfly, flower bulb or seeds and flowering plant, chicken egg (real or plastic) and a chick (real or toy). Place the chrysalis, bulb/seeds, and egg on a front table. Place the other items out of sight, but nearby. Write the following responsive reading. Make it colorful by using a red marker for the letters in "RESURRECTION," a black one for Group 1's lines, a green one for Group 2's lines, and an orange one for the line everyone reads.
> 1: God raised Jesus from the dead on Easter Sunday.
> 2: Although it seems unbelievable, it really happened.
> 1: Jesus rose from the dead on Easter.
> 2: Christians—go and tell people in every nation on earth the good news.
> 1: Jesus is not dead. He is alive.
> 2: Jesus loves us, forgives us, and gives us eternal life.
> All: Thank you, God. Amen.

PRESENTATION

Have the students name each item on the table. Say, "These things all look rather lifeless. Could we expect anything new and alive to come out of them?" Bring out the butterfly, flowering plant, and chick to match up with each thing as the students name them. Say, "Each of these things produces something new and alive." Write "RESURRECTION." Explain that this big word means "coming to life again after dying." The first objects they looked at looked rather dead, but SURPRISE! something exciting and alive came from each one. Ask the students if they remember where Jesus' body was put after he died on the cross. (In a tomb.) "Would you expect something alive and exciting to come out of a tomb where a person was buried? (No.) But what happened in the tomb on Easter? (God brought Jesus back to life after three days.)" Continue, "God promised this would happen. We call it 'the resurrection'—Jesus came back to life. God had a very special reason for making this happen. Does anyone know that reason?" (The desired answer in relationship to this discussion is, to give everyone who believes in Jesus the gift of eternal life, but the forgiveness of sins may also be part of the answer.) Invite the students to listen to the Bible text. Briefly discuss how each of the objects on display is related to the springtime of the year, and because new life comes from them they help us remember how Jesus came to life and brought a new kind of life in the resurrection.

PRAYER Divide the group in two. Assign Group 1 the black lines; Group 2 the green lines. Have everyone read the last line.

RELATED OPENINGS 19, 35

SHEEP AND SHEPHERDS   46

TEXT   Psalm 23:1a; John 10:1-5

PREPARATION   Tape-record yourself and another adult giving "Simon Says"-type directions, such as, "Hop on one foot." The other person's voice should be distinctly different from yours. Record three to five minutes of such directions, alternating speakers after every two or three phrases. Bring the tape and tape player. Write "The Lord is my shepherd."

PRESENTATION

Read Psalm 23:1a. Ask, "If the Lord is the shepherd, who are the sheep?" *(We are.)* Read John 10:1-5. Ask, "How can the sheep tell which person is their shepherd?" *(By the voice.)* Introduce the game "The Shepherd Says." Explain that two different voices will be giving directions. They should obey only your voice because you are the shepherd. They should not obey the other voice. Play the game. If someone makes a mistake, allow the player to continue playing. After playing, discuss: Who is our shepherd? *(Jesus.)* How do we hear what Jesus wants us to do? *(We hear from the Bible, from our church, our families, etc.)* Is it easy to follow what Jesus tells us to do? *(Not always.)* What other voices sometimes confuse us? *(Friends, other children, television, etc.)*

PRAYER Point to "The Lord is my shepherd." Ask the students to read that line each time you pause in this prayer: "Lord, when we're having trouble deciding which way to go, help us remember *(pause)*. When we're having trouble knowing who to follow, help us remember *(pause)*. When we're tempted to do something wrong, help us remember *(pause)*. Amen."

RELATED OPENING 51

STEWARDSHIP   47

TEXT   Deuteronomy 16:17 (In Today's English Version, use 16:16b-17)

PREPARATION   Bring some coins, a clock, a can of food or some clothing, and a globe. Set these on a front table. On separate sheets of paper, write the letters for "STEWARDSHIP." Fasten them, in order, in front of your opening area, with the blank side facing out. Write the Bible text.

PRESENTATION

Have the students identify each item on the table. Say, "The coins stand for our money, the clock represents our time, the food/clothing symbolizes our belongings, and the globe represents our earth. All of these objects have something to do with this mystery word." Invite the students to guess the word, one letter at a time. Whenever they correctly guess a letter, turn over the paper or papers with that letter. Once the word is discovered, ask what "STEWARDSHIP" has to do with the items on the table. Help the students understand that our money, time, possessions, and earth are gifts from God. God expects us to take good care of them and to share them with others. Stewardship is the act of caring for and sharing what belongs to God. Invite the students to read aloud the Bible text. Ask, "What does this verse tell us to do?" Discuss ways we can care for and share our money, time, possessions, and the earth.

PRAYER   Invite the students to write a group prayer concerning stewardship. Read it together.

RELATED OPENINGS   56, 67, 70, 90–101

THANKSGIVING 48

TEXT   Psalm 92:1

PREPARATION   Several weeks before this opening, invite the students to bring in pictures of things for which they're thankful. Emphasize that "things" can include love, happiness, joy, forgiveness, and friendship as well as objects. Create an art display with their pictures in the opening area. Write the Bible text on a large, colorful piece of paper. Choose several songs about giving thanks.

PRESENTATION

As the students arrive, direct them to the display of pictures. Encourage them to explain their drawings to one another. Call everyone together. Invite them to read the Bible text. Sing the songs you chose. After singing, ask the students to name some things for which they're thankful.

PRAYER   Tell the students there will be a time of silence at the end of this prayer when they can thank God silently: "Lord, you've given us so much. *(Read the list. Then leave a time of silence.)* Thank you, Lord. Amen."

RELATED OPENINGS   25, 69

TRINITY 49

TEXT   2 Corinthians 13:13

PREPARATION   Draw a larger version of the Trinity symbol shown here. Bring an apple, a knife, a cutting board, and a marker. Write the Bible text. Add "Amen" at the end. Place the items on a front table.

PRESENTATION

Write "Trinity." Say, "This is a word that describes God." Underline the "Tri" portion of the word. Ask, "How many wheels does a tricycle have? *(Three.)* How many sides does a triangle have? *(Three.)*" Explain that "tri" means three. We believe in one God who is made up of three persons. Name them, Father, Son, and Holy Spirit, or the names most commonly used in your church. Say, "It's hard to understand how three can be one, so I'm going to use this apple to explain the Trinity." Hold up the apple. "This is one apple. When I cut it, you'll see that this one apple has three parts." Cut it in half. Invite them to name the three parts. Ask, "How is each part important? *(The skin protects the fruit. The flesh nourishes people, plants, and animals. The seeds grow new plants.)* Who are the three persons in the Trinity? What does each do? *(God the Creator creates, protects, and judges. God our Savior forgives and nourishes us with his love. God the Spirit gives us the power to tell others about Jesus.)*" Point to the Trinity symbol. Explain that this symbol stands for God. Have the students look for the three parts that go together to make the symbol. Write the name of one person of the Trinity (Father, Son, and Holy Spirit) in each part.

PRAYER   Read the Bible text together.

RELATED OPENING   62

HOLY LAND

TEXT   Genesis 12:1

PREPARATION   Display a map of the Holy Land and a globe. Invite someone who has visited or lived in the Holy Land to tell the students about his or her experience. Emphasize the need for an age-appropriate presentation. Your guest might want to bring slides, a video, or objects. Provide whatever equipment is needed.

PRESENTATION

Read the Bible text. Point to the map and say, "This is the land to which God led Abram. Who can find this land on the globe?" After someone has found it, introduce your guest. Allow time for questions after the presentation.

PRAYER   "Lord, thank you that *(name of guest)* came to tell us about the Holy Land. Amen."

SUGGESTED FOLLOW-UP   Write a group thank-you to your guest.

SHEPHERDS 51

TEXT   Chosen by presenting group

PREPARATION   Approximately two months before you plan to do this opening, ask one of the teachers, or youth group leaders, if their students would be willing to research the lives of shepherds in Bible times and create their own skit, or puppet show, to present to the students. Have them include a prayer and Bible text about shepherds. (You may need to explain how to use a Bible concordance.)

PRESENTATION

Introduce the students who are presenting the opening. Thank them after their presentation.

PRAYER (Chosen by presenting group.)

RELATED OPENING 46

FOODS

52

TEXT 1 Samuel 25:18; Deuteronomy 8:8; Matthew 14:17

PREPARATION Choose several of these foods for the students to taste, touch, smell, and see: bread, honey, roasted lamb, grapes, raisins, figs or dried figs, wheat, barley, pomegranates, olives, olive oil, dates, onions, cheese, cooked lentils, cucumbers, melons, salt, or fish. Cut foods to be tasted into bite-size pieces. Put each food in a separate container. Bring plates, forks or spoons, and napkins. If you plan to serve grape juice, bring cups. Choose a table grace.

PRESENTATION

Ask, "What are your favorite foods?" After a brief discussion, ask, "Did people who lived in the days of Abraham, or King David, or Jesus eat these foods? What did they eat?" List the foods they mention. When they run out of ideas, invite a volunteer to read aloud each Bible verse. Add any new foods to the list. Say, "Today you will see, smell, taste, and touch some of the foods eaten during Bible times." Clearly indicate which foods are to be eaten and which are only to be smelled or touched. Pass around plates and other supplies. Say, or sing, a table grace. While the students are eating, you might want to mention how some of the foods were grown and prepared.

PRAYER Say a favorite table grace.

RELATED OPENINGS 53, 94, 96

BREAD

53

TEXT Matthew 4:4

PREPARATION Bring an unsliced loaf of bread, some unleavened bread, and two large containers. Write the words of the Lord's Prayer.

PRESENTATION

Show the two kinds of bread and ask, "How are these two the same? How are they different? (One has yeast to make it rise and the other doesn't.) Write the words *leavened* and *unleavened*. Explain what they mean and ask the students to tell you which of the two breads is leavened and which is unleavened. Tell the students that in Jesus' day the people ate both kinds of bread. Break the loaf of bread into bite-size chunks and place the pieces into one container. Break the unleavened bread into pieces and place them in the other container. Pass them around and invite the students to taste one of each. While they are eating, share some of the following information: In Jesus' time, bread was considered the main food at any meal. In fact, the word *bread* was often used to mean "food." Bread was always broken with the hands, never cut with a knife. The term *breaking bread* often meant "eating a meal." Women made the bread. People were allowed to eat only unleavened bread during Passover. Say, "Jesus knew how important bread was to his people, but he also knew that there was something even more important. Listen to find out what it is." Read the Bible text. Discuss its meaning.

PRAYER Pray the Lord's Prayer together. Ask them to listen for the part about "bread."

RELATED OPENINGS 17, 29, 38, 52

WATER 54

TEXT Isaiah 58:11

PREPARATION Find pictures of the Holy Land that show how dry it is. Try to find pictures of a well, women carrying water in jugs, women drawing water, women gathered at a well, or shepherds and their sheep at a well.

PRESENTATION

Say, "I'm thinking of something that's more precious than gold. I'll give you some clues: Plants and animals need it. We can't live without it. People in Bible times found it in wells. We drink it." Show the group the pictures of the Holy Land. Have them notice how dry it is. Explain that even in a dry place like the Holy Land there's water under the ground. Much of it comes from melting snow, running off the mountains to the north of the Holy Land. The people dug wells to reach this water. Ask if anyone has seen a well. If so, have them describe it. Say, "Several Bible stories mention water and wells. Sometimes there was only one well for an entire village. Whose job was it to carry the water from the well? How did they carry it? When did they carry it?" Let the students share what they know. Show pictures that relate to what is being discussed. Add all, or some, of this information: The women went to the well early in the evening, just before the sun went down, when the temperatures were cooler. They carried leather buckets and long ropes for pulling up the water. After pouring the water into clay pots, they balanced them on their heads and walked home. If larger amounts of water were needed, men carried the water in the skins of goats or sheep that were sewed to make big bags. When the streams went dry, the shepherds visited the well at noon to water their flocks. Say, "Water was precious to the people in Bible times. When they heard this verse, they knew how much God loved them." Read the Bible text.

PRAYER "Lord, we praise you for your great love. Thank you for your guidance and protection. Help our faith grow like a well-watered garden. Amen."

HOUSES 55

TEXT Mark 14:12-15

PREPARATION Bring four boxes: two shoe boxes that are about the same size; a large box that will hold both shoe boxes; and a box about one-third the size of a shoe box. Cut down the sides of the large box until they are about two-thirds the height of the shoe boxes. Set a table in front. Put the boxes under the table. Place a black marker on the table.

PRESENTATION

Say, "Today, we're going to learn about houses in Bible times. What do you think they looked like? (Accept a variety of answers.) Just like now, there were different kinds of houses. Some people built houses of clay; others used stone. Houses in the country were usually smaller, as were the houses of poor people. We're going to build a house that might have been owned by someone who owned a business in the city." Place the big box on the table with the open part up. Say, "This is the wall around our house. In the cities, people built walls around their homes to keep out animals, robbers, noise, and dust. Each wall had one gate which was locked at night." Draw a gate in the wall. Say, "Their rooms were separated by a courtyard. This house has two rooms." Place the shoe boxes as shown. Say, "Each room had only a few windows. The larger windows overlooked the courtyard. The windows that looked out on the streets were high and small." Draw some windows. Explain that the windows were not glass. They were open with wooden bars criss-crossing them. At night, they were covered with wooden shutters. Say, "In warm weather, people liked to spend time on their roofs." As you talk, draw a simple stairway going up the courtyard side of one shoe box. Explain that richer families often built a room on their roofs. Place the smallest box upside

BIBLICAL HOUSE

down on top of the shoe box with the stairway. Draw a door and some large windows on it. "This was called the upper room. Guests commonly stayed in upper rooms. Jesus and his disciples ate the Last Supper in someone's upper room." Read the Bible text.

PRAYER   "Lord, thank you for the protection and shelter of our homes. Help us share our homes with others. Amen."

HOSPITALITY

TEXT   Romans 12:13

PREPARATION   Place some olive oil, a basin of water, a washcloth, and a towel on a front table.

PRESENTATION

Heartily welcome the students. Say, "Today we're going to learn this word." (Write *hospitality*.) Ask what it means. *(To welcome guests or strangers.)* Discuss what welcoming means. How do we welcome people at church? in our homes? Say, "In Bible times, people considered it their duty to welcome travelers into their homes. They believed travelers were guests sent by God. As a sign of hospitality, they kept their doors open during the day. Once a person was welcomed into a home, they were considered a friend. When a guest entered a house, there were special things the host did." Show the students the items on the table. Have them

guess how they were used to welcome someone, then add this information. The people in Bible times walked in sandals on dusty roads. To keep this dirt out of their homes, a guest's feet were washed by the host or the host's servant. The host poured oil on a guest's head to soothe it and to show respect. Usually olive oil was used. Then the guest was fed and given a place to sleep. Because people were expected to give travelers food and a place to sleep, there weren't many inns or hotels. Finish the discussion by saying, "Even though we don't take strangers into our homes today, God expects us to be kind to people, too." Read the Bible text.

PRAYER "Lord, help us know when it's safe for us to welcome a stranger. Open our hearts to those people you send our way. Amen."

RELATED OPENINGS 22, 23, 42, 70, 101

OCCUPATIONS 57

TEXT Psalm 104:23

PREPARATION You'll need a large open space. Write the information for each of the following occupations on a separate index card. **Carpenters** build things from wood. *Motion:* Use the edge of one hand to make a sawing motion across the palm of the other hand. **Potters** make jars from clay. *Motion:* Knead a pretend lump of clay. **Farmers** grow grain. *Motion:* Throw handfuls of pretend seeds. **Fishermen** catch fish. *Motion:* Pretend to haul in a net full of fish. **Merchants** sell things in the marketplace. *Motion:* Pretend to hold something in one hand and point to it with the other hand. **Vinedressers** care for the grape vines. *Motion:* Curl one arm to look like a basket. Pretend to pick grapes with one hand and put them in the basket. **Masons** build walls of stone. *Motion:* Pretend to lift stones to build a wall. **Scribes** write letters and contracts. *Motion:* Use one finger to make a writing motion on the palm of the other hand. **Shepherds** take care of the sheep. *Motion:* Pretend to scoop up a lamb and hold it.

PRESENTATION

Divide the students into nine groups. Arrange the groups in a large circle, leaving spaces between them. Read the Bible text. Ask, "What kinds of jobs or occupations do your moms and dads have?" Say, "Today we're going to learn about some occupations, or jobs, that people had in Bible times. Each group will get a card that tells them their occupation and a motion that shows something about the job. When you get your card, read it and practice your motion." Distribute the cards. After a few minutes, attract the students' attention and say, "We're going to play 'Bible Occupations.' The Carpenters will begin." Explain that they're to stand and say, "We're the carpenters. We build things from wood" while making their motion. Then, they sit. The second group stands, makes their motion, and tells who they are and what they do. Next, they point to the carpenters. The carpenters stand and do their motion while the second group says, "They're the carpenters. They build things from wood." Then both groups sit. The third group stands, makes their motion, and tells who they are and what they do. Then, they tell who the second and first groups are and what they do. The game continues in the same way until the last group has told what they do and has described the occupations of all the other groups.

PRAYER "Lord, thank you for all the different occupations people have. Amen."

CLOTHING 58

TEXT Colossians 3:12

PREPARATION If you have Bible costumes, bring them. Otherwise, bring pictures showing people dressed in the garments of Bible times, or cut the different clothing items from felt and display them on a flannelboard. Divide an 8½" x 11" sheet of paper into six lengthwise strips. On each strip, write the five characteristics with which God's people are to clothe themselves. (See the Bible text.) Make copies. Cut the strips apart and staple or tape them end to end to form arm bands, one per student.

PRESENTATION

Ask, "What kinds of clothes did the people in Bible times wear?" Base the rest of the presentation on their responses. As each garment is discussed, show the corresponding costume, felt piece, or picture. Include this information: (1) The tunic: worn next to the skin, worn by women and men, like a kimono, often without sleeves, knee-length. (2) The coat: worn over the tunic, always had sleeves. (3) The girdle: held the tunic and/or the coat close to the body, usually a leather belt about 6" wide, sometimes used to hold food or money. (4) The cloak: also called a robe or mantle, looser and longer than a coat, no girdle fastened around it, no sleeves, used as a blanket on cool evenings. (5) Sandals: sole of leather or wood, leather thongs fastened it to the foot. (6) The turban: always worn by men in public, protected head from intense sun, made of thick material wrapped around the head. (7) The head cloth: worn over the head by shepherds, cooler, kept in place with a coil of camel's hair. (8) Women's clothing: tunic worn as undergarment, coat worn as dress, wore veils. Ask, "Which is more important: the clothes we wear, or the way we behave?" Read the Bible text. "What does the Bible say? What behaviors does God want us to wear?" Ask what each word means. Hand out the arm bands for the students to wear after the prayer.

PRAYER Tell the students that when you pause in the following prayer, they should read aloud the behaviors God wants us to wear, listed in Colossians 3:12: "Dear God, help us wear *(pause)*. Amen."

MUSIC 59

TEXT Psalm 150

PREPARATION Research the instruments in the Bible text. Bring pictures, if available, or draw pictures of the instruments. Write out Psalm 150. Bring as many rhythm instruments as possible. (Examples: wood blocks, spoons, pan lids, kazoos.) Display them on a front table.

PRESENTATION

Invite the students to share what they know about music in Bible times. Tell them that the book of Psalms was their hymnbook. Read Psalm 150. Ask them to name the instruments in the psalm. Underline each instrument. Invite them to tell what they know about each one. Share what you know. Show any pictures you have. Let the children try out the rhythm instruments and name them. If there are students without instruments, ask them to clap their hands, snap their fingers, or slap their thighs. Explain that they are going to rewrite the psalm, replacing the names of the biblical instruments with the names of the rhythm instruments.

PRAYER Read Psalm 150:1-2. Then say, "Praise him with *(name one of the instruments)*." As each is named, the students with that instrument should play. End with "Praise him with dancing," and lead everyone in dancing. Ask them to repeat the last line, "Praise the Lord," after you.

RELATED OPENING 64

THE TEMPLE

TEXT Psalm 84:1-4

PREPARATION You will need a large open area. On the floor, with chalk or tape, lay out a rectangle three times longer than it is wide. At one end, mark off a square. Leave an entrance opening. Bring the following items, or make suitable substitutions: large kettle, barbecue grill, incense burner with or without incense, piece of cloth that is longer than the width of the rectangle, and a cardboard box containing paper replicas of two stone tablets. Place the items on a table near the rectangle. Fill the kettle with water. Bring matches if you plan to burn incense.

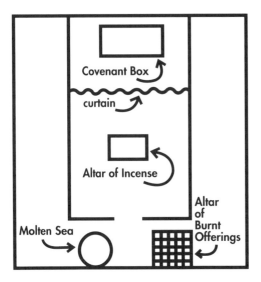

TEMPLE

PRESENTATION

Have the students sit on the floor near the rectangle. Ask them not to sit on the entrance side. Read the Bible text. Say, "This psalm is talking about the huge, beautiful temple King Solomon built in Jerusalem, long before Jesus was born. Today we're going to learn about that temple." Show them the outline of the temple and ask them to imagine walls. Explain that some worship took place inside these walls and some took place outside. Invite one student to set the kettle near the entrance. Say, "We will pretend that this is the Molten Sea, which was a large basin of water about 14 feet across and 7 feet deep. The priests washed themselves in it before going into the temple to offer sacrifice." Invite a student to place the barbecue grill next to the Molten Sea. Say, "This represents the Altar of Burnt Offering. In those days, priests sacrificed animals on this altar for the forgiveness of sins." Have another student stand in the center of the large room. Hand them the incense burner. Say, "This represents the Altar of Incense. The priests burned incense on this altar as they prayed for the people. They felt that the smoke rising from the burning incense carried their prayers to God." Point to the small square room. Say, "This room was called the Most Holy Place. The Covenant Box was kept in this room." Have a student place the box representing the Covenant Box in the room. Say, "The two stone tablets with the Ten Commandments were kept in this box." Hold up the replicas of the tablets. Explain that God's presence filled this room. The High Priest was the only person allowed to go in this room. A heavy curtain hung between the two rooms. Ask two volunteers to hold the cloth so that it hangs between the two rooms.

PRAYER "Lord, in Bible times, the temple was the place where people worshiped you. Bless the places where people worship you today. Amen."

THE SABBATH

TEXTS Exodus 20:8-11; Mark 3:1-5

PREPARATION List these Sabbath rules for later use: Women may not comb their hair. You may not light fires. You may not swat flies. You may not run or skip. You may not walk more than 1.4 miles. You may not cook. You may not plow. You may not harvest.

Read Exodus 20:8-11. Ask, "What does God say about the Sabbath? Do we have a Sabbath day? *(Sunday.)* What is different about Sunday compared to other days? *(Answers will vary.)*" The Sabbath was quite different in Bible times. Offer this information: (1) The Jewish Sabbath began at sundown on Friday and lasted until sundown on Saturday. (2) At sundown, the family lit their lamp, prayed, and shared Old Testament stories. (3) The next morning the family went to the synagogue, which was their church. The men and older boys sat in the main part of the synagogue. The women, girls, and boys under 12 sat in a gallery or balcony upstairs. God's Word was read from a scroll. (4) No work was allowed.

Read and discuss the list of rules. Say, "Pretend you're a Jewish person living at the time this story took place." Read Mark 3:1-2. Ask, "What should Jesus do?" Read Mark 3:3-4. Ask, "Why didn't the people answer? What would you have said? What do you think Jesus did?" Read verse 5. Ask, "Why did Jesus break a Sabbath rule? *(He wanted to heal the man's hand.)* What was he trying to show the people? *(Doing good and helping others is more important than following rules.)* How can we keep our Sabbath day holy? *(Some ideas: attend church, share God's love with someone, read the Bible, rest from our everyday work, have family devotions.)*"

PRAYER   Invite group members to pray silently, asking God to help them keep the Sabbath as a day set apart for worshiping God.

ATHANASIUS   **62**

TEXTS   Ephesians 4:5-6; John 10:30

PRESENTATION ___

Ask, "How many gods do Christians believe in? *(One.)*" Say, "Christians haven't always believed in only one God. In the early years of the Christian church, some leaders taught that Jesus was not the same God who created the heavens and the earth; that Jesus was another god, one not as important. Other Christian leaders, including one named Athanasius, argued that there is only one God. Let's see what the Bible says." Read Ephesians 4:5-6. Ask, "How many gods does this verse say there are?" Say, "Here's what Jesus said." Read John 10:30. Ask, "How many gods are there according to Jesus?" Continue, "The Roman emperor feared that this argument might cause problems, so he called the Christian leaders together. He asked them to agree on what they believed. They wrote down what they believed and called it the Nicene Creed. It stated that

there is only one God. You'd think that writing that creed would have settled the argument, but it didn't. Some leaders continued to teach that there was more than one God. Athanasius was punished by being sent away from his country five times. But he continued to say what he believed. Athanasius was an old man before the argument finally ended and Christians accepted his belief in one God." Teach the students the following words to the tune of "If You're Happy and You Know It."

If there's one God and you know it, say Amen. AMEN!
If there's one God and you know it, say Amen. AMEN!
If there's one God and you know it, and you really want to show it, if there's one God and you know it, say Amen. AMEN!

PRAYER   "Lord, thank you for people like Athanasius. Help us to believe as strongly as he did. Amen."

RELATED OPENING 49

MARTIN LUTHER

TEXT   1 John 1:9

PREPARATION   Write "FORGIVENESS" on several pieces of paper. Choose a hymn by Martin Luther.

PRESENTATION

Ask the students to raise their hands if they did something wrong this past week. Say, "Great! You need some of this forgiveness I have for sale." Hold up the papers. "One forgiveness costs $500. Who wants to buy some?" Wait for the students to react. If no one tells you that forgiveness can't be bought, ask, "Can you buy forgiveness? How do you get forgiveness?" Read the Bible text. Continue, "You probably thought I was crazy trying to sell forgiveness. But more than 400 years ago, when Martin Luther lived, the church sold forgiveness. They did other things, too, with which Martin Luther didn't agree. As a professor of the Bible at the university in Wittenberg, Germany, Martin Luther decided to start a debate. He thought that once all the professors began looking for answers in the Bible, they would realize how wrong these practices were. So, on October 31, 1517, he nailed a list of 95 arguments to the door of his church. To his surprise, none of the professors wanted to argue against him. Instead, someone printed copies and gave them to the people. Many agreed with Martin Luther's ideas. When the pope learned what Martin Luther had written, he wanted him killed. The following years were dangerous ones for Martin Luther, but he managed to stay alive. He translated the Bible from Latin into German, taught students, wrote books, and composed hymns. His ideas swept across Europe. He gained many followers who broke away from the Roman Catholic Church. They became known as Lutherans." Sing or listen to one of Martin Luther's hymns.

PRAYER   "Thank you, Lord, for the faith and courage of people like Martin Luther. Help us speak out against wrong practices. Amen."

JOHANN SEBASTIAN BACH

TEXT   1 Chronicles 16:23-24

PREPARATION   Invite some students or members of your church to play portions of some of Bach's pieces or get cassette recordings of them. Give each musician a time limit. Ask what they need in order to perform. Write the Bible text as a responsive reading for two groups.

PRESENTATION

Invite the students to raise their hands if they've heard of Johann Sebastian Bach. Ask them to share what they know about Bach. Add some, or all, of the following information. Johann Sebastian Bach was born in Germany in 1685. Johann played the piano and organ, sang in the church choir, and composed music. At the top of every piece of music he composed, he wrote the letters *J.J.* which stand for the Latin words *Jesu Juva*, meaning "Jesus help me." At the end of many pieces, he wrote *S.D.G.* In Latin, those letters stand for *Soli Deo Gloria*, meaning "To God alone the glory." Bach believed that his musical abilities came from God. He dedicated his life to glorifying God through his music. Read the Bible text responsively. Introduce the musicians and invite them to play. Thank them for performing.

PRAYER   "Lord, thank you for people like Johann Sebastian Bach and these musicians who use their talents to glorify you. Make us aware of the abilities you've given us. Give us opportunities to use them to glorify you. Amen."

RELATED OPENINGS 59, 87

MARY JONES

TEXT   Acts 12:24

PRESENTATION _____

Hold up a Bible and say, "Pretend that you wanted your own Bible, but your family couldn't afford to buy you one. What would you do?" When someone suggests earning money, say, "That's what Mary Jones decided to do. She was a girl who lived about 200 years ago in Wales, which is near England. How long do you think it took her to save enough?" After they have responded, say, "It took her six years to earn enough money to buy a Bible." Ask the students how far they would walk to buy a Bible. Then continue, "Early one morning Mary started walking toward the little town of Bala. The Reverend Thomas Charles lived there. She'd been told that he had some Bibles printed in Welsh, the language she

knew." Invite them to guess how far she walked. Say, "After walking 28 miles, she arrived at his house. How do you think she felt when he told her he didn't have any more Welsh Bibles?" Allow time for responding. Then say, "Rev. Charles felt so sorry for Mary that he gave her one of his own Bibles. Later, he told some people in London about how hard Mary had worked to get a Bible. They decided that there were probably lots of people like Mary Jones, people who wanted a Bible, but couldn't afford or find one. So, they started a Bible Society. Its mission was to print Bibles in many different languages and give them to anyone who wanted their own Bible." Read the Bible text.

PRAYER   "Lord, sometimes we take our Bibles for granted. Help us to see what a precious gift your Word is. Amen."

RELATED OPENINGS   77–89

HARRIET TUBMAN

TEXT   Nahum 1:7

PREPARATION   Choose an African American spiritual about Moses, freedom, or the promised land.

PRESENTATION _____

Write "Moses." Have the students share what they know about Moses. If they don't mention that Moses was the one who led God's people out of slavery in Egypt, do so. Say, "In the mid-1800s, people called Harriet Tubman 'The Moses of her people.' She was an escaped slave who returned to the South again and again to rescue more than 300 of her people. Even though there was a $40,000 reward for her capture, no one ever caught her." Ask, "Who do you think protected Harriet from natural dangers and people who wanted to capture her?" Read the Bible text. Say, "On one trip, Harriet discovered that the man who usually fed and hid her group had been

arrested for helping runaway slaves. Her exhausted, hungry group had traveled all night. Soon it would be day. Where could they hide? Did the stranger living in her friend's house suspect that she was a runaway slave? Would he send someone looking for them? Harriet prayed, asking God to protect and rescue them. Then, she remembered an island in a swamp just outside of town. All day they lay on the cold, wet ground, hidden by the tall grass. All day Harriet prayed that God would rescue them. Toward evening a man walked past the swamp. He seemed to be talking to himself, but Harriet soon realized that he was telling them where to find a wagon.

When night fell, Harriet found the wagon filled with food and supplies. Soon they were on their way. Harriet had no idea how the man discovered them, but she was certain God had sent him in answer to her prayers." Sing the song you chose.

PRAYER   "Lord, when we're in trouble, remind us of Harriet Tubman. Give us faith that you'll protect and rescue us. Amen."

RELATED OPENINGS   36, 44

TOYOHIKO KAGAWA 67

TEXT   John 15:12

PREPARATION   Choose some songs about love.

PRESENTATION

Ask, "What's a slum?" Explain that a slum is a rundown area of a city where many poor people live. Say, "Toyohiko Kagawa (toh-yoh-hee-ko kah-gah-wah) was a seminary student in Japan. A seminary is a school where people learn how to teach others about God. During the day, Toyohiko studied at the seminary. After classes, he preached in the slums. Every night, he returned to the seminary to sleep. Some of the people living in the slum wouldn't listen to Toyohiko. Why should they listen to someone who had enough to eat and a comfortable place to sleep?" Ask the group how they think Toyohiko solved that problem. Continue, "Toyohiko realized that he would have to live among the poor people. So he moved into a windowless shack in the slums. Even though it was only six feet square, several people moved in with him. They listened as he told them about Jesus. After Toyohiko graduated, he spent the rest of his life helping the poor people of Japan." Read the Bible text. Discuss how Toyohiko Kagawa's life was an example of the love described in this verse. Sing the songs.

PRAYER   "God, when you wanted to show us your love, you came to earth to live among us. When Toyohiko Kagawa wanted to show your love to the people in the slums, he went to live among them. Help us remember these examples as we try to share your love with others. Amen."

RELATED OPENINGS   42, 90–101

MARY McLEOD BETHUNE 68

TEXT   1 Corinthians 13:13

PREPARATION   Bring $1.50. Write the following prayer. Leave plenty of space under each phrase.
                        Lord, give us faith, so we can . . .
                        Give us hope, so we can . . .
                        Give us love, so we can . . .
                        Lord, thank you for giving us faith, hope, and love. Amen.

PRESENTATION

Hold up the money. Ask, "What could you do with $1.50? Listen to find out what one woman did. Mary McLeod Bethune wanted to learn to read and write, but there were no schools for black children where she lived. Finally, when Mary was 11, a school that she could attend opened just five miles from her home. Her parents needed most of their 17 children at home to help in the fields, but they decided to let Mary go to school. Years later, after she had become a teacher, Mary heard there were no schools for black children in Daytona Beach, Florida, so she moved there with only $1.50 and faith that God would help her dream come true. In a few months, with the help of many people, Mary's school opened. The school Mary began in 1904 is now a college. During her life, she also founded a hospital that treated black people and served in the government under President Franklin Roosevelt. There is a statue of Mary McLeod Bethune in Washington, D.C. Around the base are her last words: 'I leave you faith, I leave you hope, I leave you love.' " Read the Bible text. Discuss how faith, hope, and love helped Mary.

PRAYER Have the students complete the prayer. Pray it together.

RELATED OPENINGS 36, 42

CORRIE TEN BOOM 69

TEXT 1 Thessalonians 5:18

PREPARATION Ask a woman who enjoys storytelling to read pages 179-181 and pages 189-190 in *The Hiding Place* by Corrie ten Boom (with John and Elizabeth Sherrill, Chosen Books, 1971). Have her come as Corrie ten Boom and tell the story of the fleas. Ask her to include the Bible text in her story.

PRESENTATION

Invite the students to tell you some things they complain about. List their complaints. Say, "Today we're going to meet Corrie ten Boom. Actually, she's not the real Corrie ten Boom, but you can pretend she's Corrie. Corrie lived in Holland with her father and sisters. When German soldiers invaded Holland before World War II, the Jewish people living there were in danger because the German government did not like Jewish people. Corrie and her family, who were Christians, hid some Jewish people in a secret room in their house. Then, one day, the German police discovered their secret. Corrie and her sister, Betsy, wound up in Ravensbruck, a prison." Introduce "Corrie ten Boom." After the presentation, thank Corrie for sharing her story. Discuss what she learned. Examine the complaints list. What good might be seen in some of the items on the list? For example, perhaps making your bed isn't so bad. You can be thankful you have a place to sleep.

PRAYER Invite the students to pray silently, thanking God for something they complain about. Have them ask God to show them the good in that situation or thing. Conclude by saying "Amen."

RELATED OPENING 48

MOTHER TERESA 70

TEXT Luke 18:22

PREPARATION Find a book or magazine article about Mother Teresa that has her photograph. Write this prayer: Lord, thank you for people like Mother Teresa. Fill our hearts with love for those in need. Help us serve them. Amen.

PRESENTATION

Read the Bible text. Say, "Today we're going to learn about a woman who gave up her possessions and has spent her life helping the poor. Her name is Mother Teresa." Show the photograph. Ask, "What do you know about her?" Fill in the discussion with this information. When she was 12, in Albania, Mother Teresa heard a missionary speak about his work in India. From that day on, she dreamed of going to India as a missionary. At 19, she became a Catholic sister. She moved to India where she taught high school. After several years, she decided to quit teaching so she could spend all her time helping the poor. Other women joined her. They called themselves the Missionaries of Charity. Mother Teresa's love for the poor inspired many people to donate money. With it, she built schools, hospitals, and orphanages. She inspired others to become missionaries. There are now Missionaries of Charity in many countries. In 1979, she won the Nobel Peace Prize. Ask, "Who are the people that need help in our community? How could we help them?"

PRAYER   Read the prayer together.

RELATED OPENINGS   90–101

MARTIN LUTHER KING JR.

TEXT   Matthew 5:44

PREPARATION   Invite some adults and teenagers to dramatize this incident. A black teenage boy and his black teacher rode the bus to a speech contest about 100 miles away. The boy won second place. They had traveled about 10 miles on their way home when some white people boarded the crowded bus. Since there weren't enough empty seats, the bus driver asked the boy and his teacher to give up their seats. The two of them stood for nearly 90 miles even though they had paid the same amount for their tickets.

PRESENTATION

Introduce the skit. After the skit, ask, "How do you think the boy felt?" Allow time for sharing. Say, "When that boy grew up he helped change the laws so that nonwhite people would have the same rights as white people. His name was Martin Luther King Jr." Have the students share what they know about him. Include the following information. Martin Luther King Jr. was a Baptist minister who believed in nonviolent protest. That means disagreeing in peaceful ways. He made a famous speech in which he said, "I have a dream of a time when all God's children, black men and white men, Jews and Gentiles, Protestants and Catholics, will be able to join hands and sing." He won the 1964 Nobel Peace Prize when he was only 35 years old. Read the Bible text.

PRAYER   Invite the students to close their eyes and think of someone who has treated them unfairly. Ask them to pray silently, asking God to help them forgive and show love to that person. Conclude by saying, "Thank you, God, for people like Martin Luther King Jr. who show us how you want us to live. Help us work to change things that are unfair. Amen."

RELATED OPENINGS   37, 42

DESMOND TUTU   72

TEXT   Micah 4:3

PREPARATION   Write the following list and place it where the students will see it as they enter. (1) Boys may not sit in chairs. (2) Boys must sit in back, behind everyone else. (3) Boys may not eat cookies (or whatever delicious treat you bring). Invite some adults to enforce the rules. Ask one adult to give treats to the girls as they enter. Leave space behind the chairs for the boys to sit.

PRESENTATION ————————————————————————————————

As the students enter, assist them in following the rules. When it's time to begin, ask, "How do you feel about the new rules?" Give both groups time to share. Then, invite the boys to sit with the others. Give them the same treat you gave the girls. Say, "Today we're going to learn about a man named Desmond Tutu. He was born in South Africa. Because he was black, he had to live in a poor black township near Johannesburg, the richest city in South Africa. His family didn't have much money. Their small home didn't have electricity or plumbing." In 1948, the South African government passed many antiblack laws. Black people couldn't go to the same school, ride the same transportation, use the same public toilets, or sit on the same

benches as white people. In 1955, the government forbade anyone to teach black children anything that might help them learn. Ask, "How do you think the black people felt? If you had been one of them, how would you have reacted? Desmond Tutu was a teacher at the time that law was passed. Since he could no longer teach, he became a priest. Today Desmond Tutu holds the highest position in the South African Anglican Church. Over the years, he has tried to help people of all races to understand that they can live together in peace. He won the Nobel Peace Prize in 1984. In his acceptance speech, he mentioned this verse from the Bible." Read Micah 4:3. Point out that in both cases a weapon is turned into a farm tool, a symbol of peace.

PRAYER   "Lord, thank you for people like Desmond Tutu who teach us to love others and to solve our problems peacefully. Amen."

RELATED OPENINGS   26, 42

ROBERT HILL   73

TEXT   Hebrews 13:16

PREPARATION   Write the Bible text.

PRESENTATION ————————————————————————————————

Ask, "Who was Albert Schweitzer?" Have them tell what they know. Share this information: Albert Schweitzer spent his life as a missionary doctor in Africa. In 1953, at the age of 78, he won the Nobel Peace Prize. Many people were inspired to send money and supplies so he could continue helping people in Africa. Continue, "A 13-year-old from Georgia was one of those people. Robert Hill wanted to give Dr. Schweitzer a bottle of aspirin, but he couldn't figure out how to get it to Africa. At last, he wrote to an Air Force lieutenant stationed in Italy. He asked if the lieutenant could fly over Dr. Schweitzer's hospital and drop the bottle of aspirin.

The lieutenant told the Italian and French newspapers about Robert's request. The newspapers encouraged their readers to show the same generosity as Robert Hill. As a result, they raised $400,000 for supplies for Dr. Schweitzer's hospital. When the supplies were flown to Africa, Robert Hill and his bottle of aspirin went with them. Imagine how excited Robert must have been when he personally handed the bottle of aspirin to Dr. Schweitzer." Invite the students to read the Bible verse. Encourage them to tell how they've helped others.

PRAYER   "Lord, teach us to see the needs of others. Help us to do what we can. Amen."

RELATED OPENING   91

JONI EARECKSON TADA

TEXT   Romans 8:28

PRESENTATION

Ask, "What activities do you like?" Write a list. Then, cross off everything that requires the use of arms and/or legs. Say, "Today we're going to learn about a woman named Joni Eareckson Tada (pronounce *Joni* like Johnny). Joni loved to ride horses, ski, and swim. Then, one day, when she was only 17, she had a diving accident that paralyzed her from the neck down." Discuss how your life would change if you couldn't use your arms or legs. Refer to your list. Say, "Joni was miserable. She couldn't do many of the things she loved to do. She felt useless. At one low point, she even asked God to let her die. After awhile, Joni realized that God loved her, in spite of the hard changes in her life. She began to study the Bible. Here's a Bible verse that helped her as she struggled to begin a new life."

Read the Bible text. Invite the students to think of some good that might come from being in Joni's situation. Say, "Joni's faith grew stronger. She learned to draw by holding a pen in her mouth. Her art impressed many people. Articles about her appeared in newspapers and magazines. She made television appearances. Other people with physical disabilities were encouraged by her cheerful courage. Joni became a well-known artist, speaker, author, and singer. In 1979, she founded Joni and Friends, a Christian organization dedicated to ministering to the needs of people with disabilities. God has given Joni many opportunities to tell others about Jesus. Joni learned that by trusting God, a person can live a fulfilling life without the use of their arms or legs."

PRAYER   "Lord, thank you for people like Joni Eareckson Tada who help us understand that God can bring good out of every situation. Amen."

SUGGESTED FOLLOW-UP   Discuss: Are people in wheelchairs able to worship in our church? If not, what changes would have to be made?

KATHRYN KOOB

TEXTS   John 14:26; Matthew 28:20b; Psalm 46:1; Deuteronomy 31:6

PREPARATION   Write out the above Bible verses.

PRESENTATION

Invite the students to recite any Bible verses they know by heart. Ask, "When might it be important to know a Bible verse by heart?" Discuss some situations in which you might not have a Bible available, or might not be physically able to use a Bible. Say, "Today we're going to learn about a woman named Kathryn Koob. In 1979, Kathryn and 51 other Americans working in Iran were taken as prisoners by a large group of Iranian students. Kathryn spent the first night in a small room all by herself, listening to the screams of the angry crowd. She wondered what would happen to her and the other Americans. She felt scared and alone. Then, she remembered two Bible verses that she'd learned when she was young." Point to John 14:26 and

Matthew 28:20b. Discuss how these verses might have helped. Continue, "When Christmas came, Kathryn made a nativity scene out of scraps of paper. It had an angel, Mary, Joseph, the manger, and the baby Jesus. Several of the students who guarded her asked her to tell them about Jesus' birth. One student gave her a tinsel star which she hung over the manger. Another student gave her a Bible. That Bible became Kathryn's most prized possession. Kathryn and the other Americans were prisoners for 444 days. During that time, Kathryn wondered if she would ever see her family again. Every time she became depressed, God reminded her of a Bible verse that gave her hope." Point to Psalm 46:1 and Deuteronomy 31:6. Discuss how these verses might have helped Kathryn. Say, "During the time Kathryn was a prisoner, her faith grew stronger. She learned to trust God in all situations. She especially thanked God for her parents, pastor, and church school teachers who had taught her about God and insisted that she memorize Bible verses."

PRAYER "Lord, thank you for people like Kathryn Koob who remind us how important it is to read and study the Bible. Inspire us to do the same. Amen."

RELATED OPENINGS 77–89

HOMETOWN HEROES 76

TEXT Matthew 5:16

PREPARATION Use this opening after learning about other heroes in this section. Choose songs about letting your light shine, or helping others.

PRESENTATION

Ask, "Who are the faith heroes in our community?" Each time someone suggests a name, ask them to tell why they chose that person. List the names. Read the Bible verse aloud. Point to the list and ask, "How are these people doing what this verse says?" Sing the song(s) you chose.

PRAYER For each person on your list, pray, "Thank you, God, for (person's name)." Then, add a sentence for each one, asking God to help them continue (mention what they do) or thanking God for (what they've done). End with an "Amen."

SUGGESTED FOLLOW-UP Invite some of your community faith heroes to talk with the students.

GOD'S WORD I 77

TEXT Romans 15:4

PREPARATION Bring a stopwatch and a picture of a scroll. Choose a song about the Bible.

PRESENTATION

Ask, "Who can tell us a story about something that happened to your parents or grandparents before you were born?" After someone has shared something, ask, "How did you learn that story? Is it written down?" Make the point that most families have stories they pass down. Say, "Before writing was invented, telling stories was the only way people learned stories. That was the way God's family passed along the stories of what God had done. They told their children and grandchildren about Adam and Eve, Noah, and Abraham. When people began writing, they wrote these stories down. In Jesus' day these stories were written on scrolls." Show the picture of the scroll. Explain that scrolls were handwritten. Invite an older student to write in their neatest writing the Bible text as you dictate it. Time how long it takes. Figure out how many words that person would be able to write in one hour. Have the students imagine how long it would take to write all the words in the Bible in their best handwriting. Say, "Handwritten scrolls took a long time to write. They also took up a lot of room." Place a Bible flat on a front table and hold up all the pages in Romans. Say, "See how much space the book of Romans takes. When it was written in a scroll, it was about 13 feet long. A few hundred years after Jesus' time, people began making something that looked more like a book. But these books were handwritten, so there were not very many of them and they were expensive. In the mid-

1400s, a man named Gutenberg invented the printing press. That is when Bibles began looking more like our Bibles. Since they did not take as long to produce, there were more made and they were less expensive. More people could afford to buy their own Bible." Sing the song you chose. Read the Bible text in unison.

PRAYER   "Lord, thank you for giving us your Word in the Bible. Teach us as we study it. Give us the hope you promised. Amen."

GOD'S WORD II   78

TEXTS   2 Timothy 3:16; John 3:16

PREPARATION   Bring a book or magazine that contains stories or poems by various writers. Write the following on a large sheet of paper: "Sic enim Deus dilexit mundum, ut Filium suum unigenitum daret, ut omnis, qui credit in eum, non pereat, sed habeat vitam aeternam. Secundum Ioannem 3:16."

PRESENTATION

Hold up a Bible and ask, "What is this? Who wrote it?" After they've responded, say, "This collection of books called the Bible was written by about 40 people. The earliest books were written more than 1000 years before the last books were written." Hold up the book or magazine and say, "Here's a collection of stories written by different people." Open it and point out the various titles and authors. "How is the Bible different from this book?" Give them time to share ideas. Say, "I'm going to read a Bible verse that will explain one major difference. The word *scripture* is used in this verse. That's the word people used back then when they referred to the writings and stories about God and God's people." Read the verse. Invite the students to explain the major difference between the book or magazine you brought, and the Bible. Summarize by saying, "Although the Bible, or Scripture, was written by different people living at different times, God was the one who chose those people and guided them as they wrote." Hold up the Bible and say, "Some people call the Bible by another name. What is it? (*God's Word.*)" If they don't know, give clues. Point to the verse written in Latin. Ask someone to read it. Say, "This is John 3:16, written in Latin." Read the verse in English. Then say, "Hundreds of years ago, there were no Bibles written in English. In order to read the Bible, a person had to be able to read Latin or Greek. In England, it was against the law to translate the Bible into English. Luckily for us, some people broke that law. Today there are people working around the world to translate the Bible into many different languages so that someday everyone who can read will be able to read God's word for themselves."

PRAYER   Ask the students to help compose a prayer about the Bible. Pray it together.

TESTAMENTS   79

TEXT   Revelation 1:3a

PREPARATION   Have the students bring Bibles. Bring extras. Make sure you know how to pronounce the name of each book of the Bible. If not, consult someone who does. Choose a song, poem, or rap that teaches the order of the Bible books.

PRESENTATION

Distribute Bibles to those who need one. Have the students find the table of contents. Encourage them to help each other. Ask, "What are the names of the two main parts of the Bible? (*Old and New*

Testaments.)* What's the first book of the Old Testament?" Have them use the table of contents to find the page number where Genesis begins. Invite everyone to find Genesis. Ask, "What's the first book of the New Testament?" Direct them to the table of contents for the page number, then have them find Matthew. Ask, "Which testament is longer?" Invite them to count the number of books in each one. Ask, "Which testament comes first?" Returning to the table of contents, have the students point to the name of each book as you slowly pronounce, and they repeat, the names of the Old Testament books; and then, the New Testament books. Introduce the song, poem, or rap. Invite everyone to look for the name of the last Bible book, then find the page number and turn to the first page of that book. Ask them to look for the big 1, which is the chapter number, and for the little 3, which is the verse number. Read together the first part of the verse.

PRAYER "Dear God, thank you for giving us the Bible. Help us learn how to use it. Inspire us to read it often. Amen."

OLD TESTAMENT 80

TEXT   Micah 5:2,4-5

PREPARATION   You will need a large open area. Cut small squares of blue and yellow paper, five blue squares for every yellow square. Make signs that say EGYPT, WILDERNESS, PROMISED LAND, ABRAHAM, MOSES, JOSHUA, ISRAEL, JUDAH, PROPHETS, ASSYRIANS, BABYLONIANS, ASSYRIA, BABYLON. Make three paper crowns. Label each with one of these names: Saul, David, Solomon. Cut two stone tablets from paper. Practice reading the story. Find adults or teens to play Abraham, Moses, Joshua, the Prophets, Assyrians, and Babylonians. Familiarize them with their part. Give them their signs. Place EGYPT across the room from the PROMISED LAND. Place the WILDERNESS between them. Put ASSYRIA and BABYLON as far from the PROMISED LAND as possible.

PRESENTATION

Give each student a paper square. Invite them to sit on the floor. Say, "The Old Testament tells the story of how God chose a nation of people and prepared them for a Savior. Let's go on a fast trip through the Old Testament." Say, "In the beginning, God created everything, including people. The people disobeyed God and sin became part of life. But God had a plan to save his people from sin. God chose Abraham to become the father of a nation that would follow God. *(Abraham stands in front.)* God promised Abraham many children and gave them a land in which to live. *(Abraham stands in the Promised Land.)* Abraham died, but his family grew. *(Abraham leaves. Point to the students.)* You are his family, the Israelites. *(Have them stand in the Promised Land.)* The Israelites moved to Egypt after their crops wouldn't grow and they didn't have enough to eat. *(The students move to Egypt.)* After awhile, the Egyptians forced the Israelites to be their slaves. God chose Moses to be their leader. Moses led the Israelites out of Egypt and into the wilderness. *(Moses leads the students into the wilderness.)* There, God gave his people laws. *(Moses shows the stone tablets to the students.)* After 40 years, Moses died *(Moses leaves.)* and Joshua led the Israelites into the Promised Land. *(Joshua leads the students into the Promised Land.)* For many years God's people had no permanent leaders. Whenever they needed a leader, God chose a judge to lead them. But God's people decided they wanted a king. So God chose Saul as their king. *(Crown Saul.)* After Saul, David and Solomon were kings. *(Crown them.)* After Solomon died, the kingdom divided. *(Divide the students into the blue group and the yellow group.)* The northern kingdom was called Israel. *(Hand someone in the blue group the Israel sign.)* The southern kingdom was called Judah. *(Hand someone in the yellow group the Judah sign.)* The people of Israel and Judah disobeyed God. They worshiped other gods. God sent wise people called prophets to warn them to stop. *(Prophets come, shake their heads and their index fingers.)* But, the people continued to disobey. So God allowed the Assyrians to conquer Israel. They took the Israelites away to Assyria. *(Blue group moves to Assyria.)* About 100 years later, God allowed the Babylonians to conquer the disobedient people of Judah. They brought many of the people to Babylon. *(Yellow group moves to Babylon.)* About 70 years later, they were allowed to return to their land. Some did return and some stayed. *(Have part of the yellow group return to the Promised Land.)* Those in the Promised Land rebuilt their homes and cities and waited. They waited for the Messiah God had promised, the person who would save them. *(Ask the students to*

look like they're waiting.)" Gather everyone together. Invite them to sit. Ask a prophet to read Micah 5:2,4-5, one of God's promises, made to the Israelites in Old Testament times.

PRAYER "Lord, you chose people like Abraham and Moses to lead your people. Help us lead others to you. Amen."

NEW TESTAMENT 81

TEXTS Romans 10:9; Revelation 21:1-4

PREPARATION Find pictures of Jesus' birth; Jesus' baptism; Jesus ministering to people, especially healing and teaching; the Last Supper; the crucifixion; the empty tomb; the ascension; the coming of the Holy Spirit at Pentecost; the conversion of Saul; the adventures, or a map of the travels, of Paul and the other apostles; and Jesus returning to earth. Place them in the same order as they are listed.

PRESENTATION

Say, "The New Testament is the story of Jesus, our Savior. It tells the story of the beginning of the Christian church and foretells the second coming of Christ. Today we're going to look at the New Testament." Show the first picture and ask the students to tell you about it. Continue in the same way with each picture. Fill in additional information as needed. Help the students understand that God sent Jesus to die for our sins so we could be right

with God, or "righteous." Because of God's love and forgiveness, believers live with God now and after they die. God sent the Spirit to give believers the power to tell others about Jesus. The Christian church grew as believers spread the good news. Read Romans 10:9 and explain that this is the good news. Someday Jesus will come again. Read Revelation 21:1-4.

PRAYER "Lord, thank you for sending Jesus to save us from our sins. Thank you for the promise of a new heaven and a new earth. Thank you for the New Testament where we can read this good news. Amen."

CHAPTER:VERSE I 82

TEXT Psalm 86:11

PREPARATION Request that the students bring Bibles. Bring some extras.

PRESENTATION

As the students enter, invite the older students to choose seats next to the younger students. Ask them to assist the younger students in using their Bibles. Have the students turn to the beginning of Psalms. Ask them to find the large 1, then the 2, then the 3. Ask, "What do we call these sections? *(Chapters.)* How many chapters does Psalms have? *(150.)"* Invite everyone to turn to the 150th chapter of Psalms. Point out the little numbers in the chapter. Ask,

"What are these smaller sections called? *(Verses.)* How many verses does this chapter have? *(Six.)"* Write "Psalm 150:4." Say, "This is the way we indicate a verse. The word tells us the book. The first number tells us the chapter. The second number tells us the verse." Have the students find verse 4. Read it together. Write "Psalm 24:1." Ask the students to find it. Invite a volunteer to read the verse aloud. Ask the other students if that's the verse they found. Point out that the first verses in each chapter are not marked with a little 1. Write "Psalm 86:11." Give the students time to find it. Invite someone to read it aloud. Say, "The Lord teaches us through the Bible. When we read God's Word, we learn what kind of people God wants us to be."

PRAYER   Invite the students to repeat Psalm 86:11 as their prayer, adding an "Amen" to the end.

CHAPTER:VERSE II

TEXT   Psalm 32:8

PREPARATION   Write each question and its scripture reference at the top of a piece of drawing paper. You will need one paper for every four students. If you have more than 48 students, duplicate some questions, or create your own.
Genesis 6:14 What did God tell someone to make? *(Boat.)*
Joshua 6:4 What instrument did someone play? *(Trumpet.)*
Judges 14:5 What animal did someone hear? *(Lion.)*
1 Samuel 17:34 What animals did someone take care of? *(Sheep.)*
Psalm 104:17 What do these animals build? *(Nests.)*
John 21:10 What was someone told to bring? *(Fish.)*
1 Corinthians 10:16 What do we break? *(Bread.)*
Matthew 27:32 What did someone carry? *(Cross.)*
Revelation 12:3 What appeared? *(Dragon.)*
John 13:12 What did someone wash? *(Feet.)*
John 9:6 What did someone make? *(Mud.)*
1 Samuel 20:36 What was someone told to find? *(Arrows.)*
Bring drawing supplies for each group. Set up tables on which the groups can work or provide pieces of cardboard larger than the drawing paper, one per group. Have the students bring Bibles. Have extra Bibles. Invite teens or adults to help.

PRESENTATION

Distribute the extra Bibles to those students who need one. Write "Psalm 32:8." Invite the students to explain how to find that verse. Ask them to find it. Encourage them to help each other. Read the verse together. Discuss how God teaches us as we read the Bible. Invite 12 older students who are capable of finding Bible verses to be group readers. Assign each a number from 1 to 12 and a spot to work. Have them go to their areas. Ask the rest of the students to count off from 1 to 12. Have all the 1's join Reader 1, all the 2's join Reader 2, and so on. Explain that the readers will help the others find and read the Bible verse. Each group should also choose a timekeeper who will make sure their group finishes on time, an artist who supervises the drawing of the group's answer, and a presenter who will share their answer. Hold up one of the pieces of paper. Explain how they will look up the Bible verse to find the answer to the question. Then, they will draw the answer on the paper. Tell them they should plan to finish by *(a given time)*. Distribute the papers and drawing supplies. When the time is up, gather everyone together and have each group share their question and answer.

PRAYER   "Thank you, Lord, for the Bible. Teach us your ways as we read your Word. Amen."

TYPES OF WRITING 84

TEXT   Psalm 119:105

PREPARATION   On each of five sheets of paper write one of these: Law, History, Poetry, Prophecy, Wisdom. Display them in front. Ask the students to bring Bibles. Bring extras.

Point to the five signs. Say, "Here are five different kinds of writing." Help the students define each type. (*Law—rules or instructions about how to live; History—the telling of events in the order they happened; Poetry—words that help us form a picture in our minds; Prophecy—messages from God, sometimes warnings, predictions, corrections; Wisdom—words of guidance and advice.*) Tell the students you are going to read a sentence; then point to each of the five kinds of writing. The students should stand when you point to the kind of writing that the sentence or phrase represents. Read the following sentences, one by one, letting the students decide what type of writing it is before reading the next sentence: "Humpty Dumpty sat on a wall, Humpty Dumpty had a great fall." *(Poetry.)* "A penny saved is a penny earned." *(Wisdom.)* "This Jesus who was taken from you into heaven, will come back in the same way that you saw him go into heaven." *(Prophecy.)* Abraham Lincoln was the 16th president of the United States. *(History.)* No Parking. *(Law.)* If there is a difference of opinion, invite students to explain why they voted for the type of writing they did. Make sure everyone has a Bible. Then, write the following scripture references one at a time: Acts 21:4 *(History)*, Romans 12:18 *(Wisdom)*, Exodus 20:15 *(Law)*, Psalm 108:3-4 *(Poetry)*, Jeremiah 33:14 *(Prophecy)*, Leviticus 2:4 *(Law)*, Proverbs 12:25 *(Wisdom)*, Joshua 6:15 *(History)*, Psalm 119:105 *(Poetry)*. Ask the students to find the verse in the Bible. Read it together and have them vote as they did before for which type of writing it represents. Do as many as time allows. End with Psalm 119:105.

PRAYER Invite a volunteer to read Psalm 119:105 again. Pray: "Lord, may your word guide us and lead us in the ways you would have us go. Amen."

LAW 85

TEXT	Romans 3:20, 22a
PREPARATION	List some school rules that existed when you, your parents, or your grandparents were in school. Ask the students to bring Bibles to this opening. Bring additional Bibles.

PRESENTATION

Ask, "What are the rules at your school?" List their responses. Discuss why it is necessary to have rules. *(Rules help people to work and live together peaceably. They help people know what behavior is acceptable and what is unacceptable.)* Show the students your list of rules. Tell them when these rules were in effect. Ask, "Which rules are nearly the same then and now? Which are different? Why are some different?" Emphasize that as times change, some rules do not have purpose or meaning for the people living in the new times. Point out that other rules are just as important today as they were years ago. Make sure everyone has a Bible. Say, "God gave his people rules for living. We call these rules 'the law.' These laws are in the Bible. Some of these laws no longer have any meaning for us." Write "Leviticus 13:45." After the students have helped one another find that verse, invite a volunteer to read it aloud. Ask, "Would this be a good law for people today? Why do you think God made that law for people living back then? *(To keep diseases from spreading and killing large numbers of people.)*" Write "Exodus 20:1-17." After the students have located this text, invite them to listen as you read it aloud. Ask, "What do we call these laws? *(The Ten Commandments.)*" Discuss whether we should obey them today. You may need to rephrase some of the commandments into language the students will understand. Write "Romans 3:20." After the students have found it, ask someone to read it aloud. Say, "It is important to follow rules, but following all the rules perfectly does not put us right in God's sight." Have the students read the first part of verse 22.

PRAYER "Lord, thank you for giving us your laws. Help us follow them. But, most of all, give us faith to follow Jesus. Amen."

GOOD NEWS

TEXT   John 3:16

PREPARATION   Request that the students bring Bibles. Bring additional Bibles. Cut several long strips of paper. Display a sign that says "Good News." Leave room underneath it for fastening the students' "Good News" headlines. Bring the necessary supplies for fastening them, and markers. Have tables or cardboard pieces available. Write each of these Bible texts on an index card: Romans 5:8, Romans 6:23, Hebrews 9:28, 1 John 1:9, Matthew 1:21, Romans 10:9, 1 John 5:13, Romans 10:13, John 1:29, Acts 2:38.

PRESENTATION

Point to the "Good News" sign. Say, "In church we talk about the 'good news.' Another word we use is *gospel. Gospel* means 'good news.' What is this good news?" After a brief discussion, say, "We are going to divide into groups. Each group will be given a Bible verse. After reading the verse, you will write a headline that tells the good news contained in that verse. Let's try one together. Write 'John 3:16.' " Have the students find it. Read it aloud. Invite them to suggest possible headlines. *(Examples: God loves the world, God sends son to world, Believers have eternal life.)* Write their headlines on strips of paper and post them under the "Good News" sign. Divide the students into 10 groups in the same manner as described in the "Presentation" section of Opening 83. In each group there will be: a reader, a timekeeper, a headline writer, and a presenter. Give each group an index card, strip(s) of paper, and a marker. At the chosen time, call everyone together. Invite each presenter to read the group's headline and fasten it under the "Good News" sign. Invite the students to summarize the good news in a couple of sentences. *(Jesus died so that our sins would be forgiven. Because of his death we are put right with God and one day will go to live with God forever.)* Sing the song.

PRAYER   Have the students compose a prayer. Pray it together.

RELATED OPENINGS   35, 37, 42, 45

SONGS

TEXT   Chosen by leader

PREPARATION   You may want to enlist the help of your choir or music director to help you prepare and present this opening. Look through your hymnbook, worship book, or church school songbook to find songs based on texts from the Bible. Try to choose songs that are familiar to the students. You will need from three to five songs, depending on their length and the time available. Request that the students bring Bibles. Have extra Bibles on hand. Bring enough copies of whichever songbook you used so that there is one book for every two students.

PRESENTATION

Say, "The words of many songs can be found in the Bible. Today we are going to sing some of these songs and find the words in the Bible." Introduce the first song. Write the biblical reference for the song's words on your writing surface. Invite everyone to find that text in the Bible. Ask a volunteer to read it aloud, or have the students read it in unison. Sing the song again. Follow this same procedure for each song.

PRAYER   "Lord, we thank you for giving us your Word. We praise you by singing your words. Amen."

RELATED OPENINGS 59, 64

BIBLE GAME I 88

TEXT Psalm 100

PREPARATION Use this game to help the students learn sequences of Bible books. Once they have mastered a sequence, retain the last two books of the old sequence and add two books to form a new sequence. Ask the students to bring their Bibles. Provide extras. Write the first book of the first sequence on the writing surface.

PRESENTATION

Make sure everyone has a Bible. Invite the students to turn to the table of contents. Point to the name of the Bible book you wrote. Ask them to find that book in the contents. Ask, "What three books come immediately after (name of book)?" Write the three names under the first name. Have them close their Bibles and lay them close by. Ask the students to imitate what you are about to say and do. Create a three-step motion such as slap the thighs twice and clap once. Do the three-step motion, saying the first book in the sequence. Repeat the motion for the remaining three books. Do the four-book sequence

again, changing at least one step of the three-step motion. Continue in like manner until you have gone through the sequence at least four times. Then cover the sequence and ask the students to say it. If they have trouble, ask a volunteer to lead motions for the same sequence. Once the students have mastered it, write the third book of the old sequence, and have the students find the names of the next three books. Write them under the name you just wrote. Invite someone to lead the motions. Suggest movements with arms, legs, fingers, head, body, etc. Continue playing as long as time allows.

PRAYER Ask the students to find Psalm 100. Invite the younger students to read aloud verses 1 and 2; the older students to read aloud verses 3 and 4; and everyone to read verse 5. Add an "Amen" at the end.

BIBLE GAME II 89

TEXT Psalm 146:1-2

PREPARATION Have the students bring Bibles. Be sure to bring extra ones.

PRESENTATION

Write "Psalm 146:1-2." Ask the students to find it. Read it together. Say, "We are going to play 'Singing Bible Books' to help us learn the names of the books in the Bible." Choose three students and ask them to leave the room until you call them back. Mix younger and older students. Ask a volunteer to choose the name of a Bible book having more than one syllable and write it for all to see. Divide the name into syllables. Divide the students into as many groups as there are syllables. Assign one

syllable to each group. Explain that when the three students come back, each group will sing their syllable over and over to the tune of "Jesus Loves Me" or some other familiar tune. Call back the three students who left. Invite them to listen and figure out the name of the book. If necessary, they may consult a table of contents. Once they have guessed correctly, send another three students out, and begin again.

PRAYER "Lord, we praise you for giving us your Word. Help us learn how to use our Bibles. Amen."

WORLD PRAYER

90

TEXT   Psalm 117

PREPARATION   Attach a world map to a portable bulletin board, or to a double thickness of corrugated cardboard. Cut six small crosses from colored paper. Cut one large cross. Bring straight pins. Write Psalm 117.

PRESENTATION

Mention the name of a country that currently is having problems. Ask someone to point to that country on the map. Invite the students to share what they know about the problem. Ask, "Is anyone helping? What are we doing, or what could we do, to help?" Suggest that we can pray. Invite the students to compose a prayer asking God to help the people of that country. Pray the prayer. Ask a volunteer to pin a small cross on that country. Conduct the same kind of discussion for other countries. Near the end of the opening, pin the large cross on the map. Ask, "Why do you think I did that?" Say, "This cross reminds us that God loves and cares about all people everywhere."

PRAYER   As a group, read Psalm 117.

OUR PROJECT

91

TEXT   Luke 3:11

PREPARATION   Write the Bible text.

PRESENTATION

Invite the students to read the Bible text aloud. Say, "In this verse, Jesus is telling us two ways we can help other people. Today we're going to think of one way we could help somebody, and in the weeks to come, we're going to put our plan into action." Encourage the students to suggest project ideas. List their suggestions. Vote for one project. Create a plan for helping. Discuss: What needs to be done? Will we need money? What supplies will we need? How will we obtain them? When will we work on our project? You may need more than one opening to create your project plan.

PRAYER   Invite the students to compose a prayer about their project. Pray it together.

SUGGESTED FOLLOW-UP   When your plans are complete, send letters home, explaining the project. If your project is long-term, you might want to set aside time during one opening a month for project updates.

MISSIONARY VISITORS

92

TEXT   Mark 16:15

PREPARATION　　Invite a missionary to talk to your students. Ask your guest to bring pictures, objects, a map, or other items that will help the students appreciate the people he or she served.

PRESENTATION ————————————————————————————————————

Read the Bible text. Introduce your guest and invite him or her to speak to the group.

PRAYER　Invite the students to write a prayer, thanking God for their guest, praying for the people their guest served, and asking God to give each of them opportunities to serve others. Pray the prayer.

SUGGESTED FOLLOW-UP　Send a letter of thanks to the missionary, including the students' comments about what interested them most.

DISCOVERING NEEDS　　93

TEXT　　　　　　　　Isaiah 58:10

PREPARATION　　Obtain photos, slides, or videos from organizations you think your students might be interested in helping. They may take several weeks to arrive, so order them well in advance. Preview materials, so you'll know if there's anything that should be explained before the students see them.

PRESENTATION ————————————————————————————————————

Read the Bible text. Tie it in with the photos, video, or slides. Discuss the needs being met by this organization. How could the students help meet these needs?

PRAYER　Invite the students to write a prayer based on what they saw and discussed.

SUGGESTED FOLLOW-UP　Act on one of their ideas.

WORLD HUNGER　　94

TEXT　　　　　　　　Mark 8:1-8

PREPARATION　　Bring a basket, loaf of bread, and a can of fish. Set them on a front table.

PRESENTATION ————————————————————————————————————

Show the students the items. Ask, "What Bible story do you think of when you see these?" When someone mentions Jesus feeding the crowd, read Mark 8:1-4. Discuss how Jesus felt about the hungry people. Did the disciples think it was possible for them to feed all the people? What happened next? Read Mark 8:5-8. Ask, "Are there hungry people today? What would Jesus want us to do?" Brainstorm ways they could help feed hungry people around the world. List their ideas.

PRAYER　Lord, we know you care about hungry people. Help us share what we have so that people everywhere will have enough to eat. Amen.

RELATED OPENING　47

SUGGESTED FOLLOW-UP Ask the students to bring the ingredients for Multi-Bean Soup. During an opening, mix the ingredients. Assemble packages of the mix. Make copies of the recipe. Sell the packages and send the money to an organization that fights world hunger.

Ingredients for Bean Mix: Combine 10 to 20 different varieties of dried beans. (One pound equals about 2½ cups of dried beans.)

Ingredients for Herb Mix (makes over 2 cups): ½ cup dried parsley; ¼ cup cumin seeds; ⅓ cup dried savory; ½ to 1 t. cayenne pepper; 2 T. each of fennel seeds, caraway seeds, dill seeds, cracked coriander seeds, sweet basil, and dried chervil; 1 T. each of: celery seeds, dried thyme, sage, oregano, rosemary, and marjoram.

To assemble: Place 2 cups bean mix into a container. Add 2 T. herb mix, packaged separately. Attach a copy of the following recipe.

Multi-Bean Soup
Rinse the beans and place them in a large pot. Add cold water to cover by 2". Bring to boil. Boil 2 minutes. Let sit 1 hour. Drain, discarding water. Add 7 cups of chicken or vegetable stock. Add more stock as needed, to cover the beans by about 2". Add 1 bay leaf and 1 fresh or dried chili. Bring to a boil, reduce heat, cover, and simmer 1 to 3 hours or until the beans are tender. Add the herb mix. Add a variety of chopped vegetables: coarsely pureed tomatoes, sliced carrots, sliced celery with leaves, finely diced potatoes, sliced green beans. Season to taste with salt and freshly ground pepper. Add 2 t. Worchestershire sauce and 2 to 4 t. honey. Simmer covered until vegetables are tender, about 20-25 minutes. Remove the bay leaf and chili. If a thicker soup is desired, mash 1 or 2 cups of the soup and stir it into the pot. Serve hot. Excellent reheated.

GROUP ADOPTION $\boxed{95}$

TEXT   Proverbs 20:11a

PREPARATION   Call various groups in your community to find out what they do and how your students could help. Choose three groups to present to the students. Groups to consider: day care centers, nursing homes, hospital ward, shelter for the homeless, soup kitchen, prison, animal shelter, etc. Instead of providing things, the students might like to give all or a percentage of their offering to the group they decide to adopt.

PRESENTATION

Say, "There are groups in our community we can help. I'm going to tell you about three. Then, you can decide if you'd like to adopt one of them. If we do adopt a group, we'll help them throughout the year." Present each group. Ask if the students would like to adopt one of them. If so, decide which one and what you'll do first.

PRAYER Write a group prayer, asking for God's guidance as you help. Pray it together.

SUGGESTED FOLLOW-UP Set aside future openings for students to work on this project.

EMPTY BAGS

TEXT Deuteronomy 15:7-8

PREPARATION Use this opening after one where the students have decided to help an individual, or group, by bringing supplies from home. Bring one grocery sack per student. Fasten letters on the bags explaining who is being helped, what is being collected, and when the bag should be returned. Choose a song(s) about helping others.

PRESENTATION

Read the Bible text. Relate these verses to the students' project. Ask someone to explain the project to those who were absent. Review what items are being collected. Sing the song(s) you chose. Distribute the bags. When the bags are returned, give a general "thank-you" and talk about the good the donations will do; but avoid individual recognition so that those who forgot or could not afford to contribute are spared embarrassment.

PRAYER With the students, compose a prayer specific to this project. Pray it together.

LOVE KITS

TEXT 2 Corinthians 9:7

PREPARATION This opening is especially suitable after a natural disaster when kits of cleaning supplies or toiletries might be needed. Ask relief organizations to suggest what should be included in each kit. There are also groups that distribute newborn care, health, school, and other types of kits. Your pastor or church school coordinator may be able to put you in contact with one of these groups. Send for their kit content lists well in advance. A week or two before you plan to do this opening, send letters home listing the materials being collected for the kits. Since some of your students may not be able to donate items for these kits, contact other groups within your church to see if they would like to donate some. Provide the specific type of container for holding the supplies that is designated by the relief agency, or experiment to find a suitable container such as self-sealing plastic bags. Bring enough empty containers so that each student will be able to assemble at least one kit. Arrange the tables in a line so that students will be able to pick up a container at one end and add items as they walk past the tables. Prepare a place for the finished kits. Provide an area where students can sit and sing after they've assembled their kit. Choose songs appropriate to this topic. Invite some adults and teens to help.

PRESENTATION

As the students arrive, have them sort their supplies. Ask the teens and adults to assist. Read the Bible text. Discuss who the students are helping and why. Explain the assembling process and what they should do once their kit is assembled.

PRAYER Gather near the finished kits. Pray, asking God to bless the kits and the people to whom they will be given.

LOVE TAPE

TEXT   John 13:35

PREPARATION   Ask your pastor to give you the name of someone in your congregation who would appreciate receiving a love tape. A love tape from the students could include: readings of Bible verses about love, poems, songs, a "radio play" retelling a Bible story where some students are the actors and the others provide the sound effects. Bring a blank tape and tape recorder. You may need to set aside time during several openings to complete the tape.

PRESENTATION

Read the Bible text. Invite the students to tell how they show their love to other people. Hold up the blank tape. Ask if anyone has ever sent a love tape. If so, have that person tell what they recorded on their tape. Give some ideas of other things that could be included. Tell the students the name of the person your pastor suggested. Give some information about that person. Decide what that person might enjoy listening to on a love tape. Plan the tape. If time, begin taping. Finish it during subsequent openings.

PRAYER   Lord, bless this tape that we're making for *(name of person)*. May it show God's love and our love. Amen.

COLLECTION SUNDAY

TEXT   Matthew 25:31-40

PREPARATION   Contact community groups to find out what your students could collect that would aid their group in helping others. Try to include some used objects such as eyeglasses, clothing, books, toys, and magazines among the items being collected. Explain that these items will be collected *[give date(s), time, and place]*. Ask if a representative from the community group could come that day to receive the donations and answer questions. About a month in advance, send a list home with the students, telling what items are needed and by whom. Arrange for teens and adults to help. Plan where each group's collection spot will be. Make a sign for each group, include the name of the representative and the items being collected. Keep an area free for students to gather once they have finished delivering their items. Choose a variety of songs that deal with helping other people. Write Matthew 25:35-36 and Matthew 25:40. Practice reading the Bible verses, pausing at the appropriate times.

PRESENTATION

As the students arrive, help them deliver their items. As students finish, invite them to gather for singing. When everyone is together, point to the Bible verses. Say, "I'm going to read some verses that talk about helping other people. Whenever I pause, read the verse I point to." Read the Bible text, pausing when you reach one of the verses.

PRAYER   Ask the students to pray silently, asking God to bless these items and the people who will be using them. Close by praying, "Thank you, Lord, for giving us this chance to help others. Amen."

CHURCH SERVANTS

100

TEXT   Psalm 96:1-3

PREPARATION   Consult your pastor or church council as to ways elementary-aged students could help in church and during worship services. Display a list of their ideas. Choose songs about serving. Write: "Help us serve."

PRESENTATION

Show the students the list of ideas. Invite them to brainstorm other ways they could help in their church and during worship services. Add their ideas to the list. Ask students who have done some of the things on the list to share their experiences with the other students. Are there ideas the students would like to put into action? Sing the songs. Read the Bible text.

PRAYER   Point to "Help us serve." Request that the students say that phrase when you pause in this prayer: "Lord, there are many jobs that need to be done around our church; *(pause)*. There are many things that need to be done during worship services; *(pause)*. We are your servants, Lord; *(pause)*. Amen."

SUGGESTED FOLLOW-UP   Invite adults or older students who help in some of the ways listed, to come and explain how they do their jobs.

CHURCH WELCOME

101

TEXT   Matthew 10:40

PREPARATION   Read through the situations. Adapt them so that they mirror real situations that could occur in your church. Bring some simple props and/or costumes to fit the situations you plan to use.

PRESENTATION

Warmly greet the students. Read the Bible text. Ask, "What does it mean? When someone receives or welcomes you, who else are they welcoming? *(Jesus.)* So, when we welcome someone, who else are we welcoming?" Say, "Today we're going to role-play some church situations. We're going to think about all the ways the people in each situation could be welcomed. In each situation, let's also think about how Jesus would welcome these people." Before introducing each situation, invite volunteers to play the different characters. Read the situation up to, but not including, the question. Have the students role-play the situation, embellishing it to make it more real. Then, read the question and ask the audience to think of some different welcoming responses. **Situation 1:** A young man joins Mrs. Jackson in her pew. She notices that he has a bad smell about him. She also notices that during the service, he seems to have trouble finding his place in the hymnal. How could Mrs. Jackson make this man feel welcome? **Situation 2:** Joel and his dad are handing out bulletins. An older woman with a cane and a hearing aid comes in. They've never seen her before. What could Joel and his dad do to make this woman feel welcome? **Situation 3:** Amanda and her parents are waiting in line at a church potluck supper. A single mother with two active children and a fussy baby enters. The mother looks tired. Amanda has seen them at worship a few times, but doesn't know their names. How could Amanda and her family make this family feel welcome? After you've finished role-playing, think of improvements that could be made in the way your church welcomes people. Write a list of their suggestions.

PRAYER "Lord, make our church a welcoming place. Make us welcoming people. Amen."

RELATED OPENINGS 23, 42

SUGGESTED FOLLOW-UP Give the students' list of suggestions to your pastor or church council.

CHURCH SEASON COLORS AND SYMBOLS

ADVENT

Colors: Blue reminds us of the sky in which Christ will one day reappear. It's the color of hope. Purple and violet are also used. They stand for humility and penitence. Purple was the color of royalty. Jesus is the King of kings.

Symbols:

A scroll God's promise to send a Savior as recorded in Old Testament prophecies.

The tau cross This incomplete cross represents a salvation that has been promised, but has not yet come.

A lighted candle Jesus was the promised light who was to come.

Advent wreath The circle of evergreens represents God's never-ending love and eternal life. The candles represent the light that Jesus brought into the world.

Dawning sun Malachi told of the coming of the "sun of righteousness."

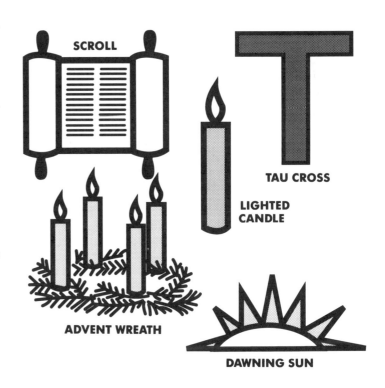

SCROLL

TAU CROSS

LIGHTED CANDLE

ADVENT WREATH

DAWNING SUN

CHRISTMAS

Color: White represents purity, light, and perfection, all characteristics of our Lord.

Symbols:

The manger Helps us remember Jesus' humble birth.

Holly leaves and bright red berries Jesus was born to die for our sins. The sharp-pointed leaves symbolize the crown of thorns. The berries represent Jesus' blood, shed for us.

Anchor cross This cross was called the cross of hope by first-century Christians. Jesus' birth brought hope to the world.

Christmas rose Isaiah prophesied that one day the desert would blossom like a rose. Jesus is compared to that rose, blossoming in a world filled with sin.

The herald angel Announced Jesus' birth to the shepherds.

MANGER

HOLLY

ANCHOR CROSS

CHRISTMAS ROSE

HERALD ANGEL

EPIPHANY

Color: Green represents life and growth. The Epiphany season emphasizes mission and the growth of God's kingdom.

Symbols:

Five-pointed star The star that led the Magi to Jesus.

Descending dove with a three-rayed nimbus The presence of the Holy Spirit at the baptism of Jesus. The three-rayed nimbus is used only with persons of the Trinity.

Three drops of water, dripping from a cockle shell Baptism. During Epiphany, we celebrate the baptism of Jesus.

Gifts of the Magi The gold, frankincense, and myrrh that the Magi gave Jesus.

The cross crosslet The central cross stands for the cross on which Jesus died. The outer crosses—the spread of Christianity north, south, east, and west. Mission is an emphasis of Epiphany.

STAR

DOVE

GIFTS OF THE MAGI

SHELL

CROSS CROSSLET

PALM BRANCHES

LATIN CROSS

PASSION CROSS

CROWN OF THORNS

CUP, GRAPES, WHEAT, BREAD

LENT

Colors: Purple and violet symbolize humility and penitence.

Symbols:

Palm branches The palm branches waved by the people on Palm Sunday when Jesus rode into Jerusalem on a donkey.

Latin cross The cross on which Jesus died.

Passion cross, also known as the "cross of suffering" Its points represent the points of the thorns, nails, and the spear.

Crown of thorns The crown of thorns the soldiers placed on Jesus' head. Jesus was the king who came to suffer for the sins of the world.

Cup, grapes, wheat, bread Symbols of Holy Communion. The cup and grapes represent Jesus' blood; the wheat and bread—Jesus' body. Both were given so our sins might be forgiven.

LAMB

LILY

BUTTERFLY

EGG

CROSS IN GLORY

EASTER

Color: White stands for our Lord's purity and perfection.

Symbols:

Lamb with banner   The lamb represents Jesus, the Lamb of God, sacrificed for the forgiveness of sins. The banner stands for Christ's victory over death.

Easter lily   The flower rises from a seemingly lifeless bulb.

Butterfly   Symbolizes the resurrection; Christ coming out of the tomb. It is also used as a symbol of eternal life.

Egg   New life. As the animal breaks out of the egg, so Jesus broke out of the tomb.

The cross in glory   The new day that dawned when Jesus triumphed over death.

PENTECOST

Colors: The red used on the first day of Pentecost represents the red of the flames that appeared over the apostles' heads. Green is used during the remainder of Pentecost. It is the color of growing plants and stands for life and growth. During Pentecost, the emphasis is on growing in faith.

Symbols:

Tongues of fire   The gift of the Holy Spirit.

A vine with grapes   Our relationship with our Lord. Our growth depends upon our staying attached to Jesus, the main stem.

Beehive   The church, working together for the good of all.

Ship   The Christian church. Christ is the captain and believers are the passengers.

St. Andrew's cross   The church. As the first disciple called by Jesus, St. Andrew represents all who have been called since.

TONGUES OF FIRE

VINE WITH GRAPES

BEEHIVE

SHIP

ST. ANDREW'S CROSS

SCRIPTURE INDEX

OLD TESTAMENT — OPENING

Genesis 12:1	50
Exodus 12:1-14	29
Exodus 20:8-11	61
Exodus 33:2a	30
Deuteronomy 8:8	52
Deuteronomy 15:7-8	96
Deuteronomy 16:17 (In Today's English Version, use 16:16b-17)	47
Deuteronomy 31:6	75
Deuteronomy 32:3	3
1 Samuel 25:18	52
1 Chronicles 16:23-24	64
Psalm 23:1a	46
Psalm 32:8	83
Psalm 46:1	75
Psalm 47:1	1
Psalm 84:1-4	60
Psalm 86:11	82
Psalm 91:11	30
Psalm 92:1	48
Psalm 96:1-3	100
Psalm 96:10a	10
Psalm 100	88
Psalm 104:23	57
Psalm 117	90
Psalm 119:105	84
Psalm 122:1	24
Psalm 146:1-2	89
Psalm 148	25
Psalm 150	59
Proverbs 17:17a	23
Proverbs 20:11a	95
Ecclesiastes 3:1	2
Isaiah 7:14	5
Isaiah 9:6	9
Isaiah 58:10	93
Isaiah 58:11	54
Joel 2:28	20
Micah 4:3	72
Micah 5:2	4, 80
Micah 5:4-5	80
Micah 7:7	5
Nahum 1:7	66

NEW TESTAMENT — OPENING

Matthew 2:1a	7
Matthew 2:1-12	11
Matthew 4:4	53
Matthew 5:16	76
Matthew 5:44	71
Matthew 6:9-13	41
Matthew 10:40	101
Matthew 14:17	52
Matthew 16:21	14
Matthew 18:21-22	37
Matthew 25:31-40	99
Matthew 26:26-28	38
Matthew 28:1-3	30
Matthew 28:20b	75
Mark 1:9-11	12
Mark 3:1-5	61
Mark 8:1-8	94
Mark 8:34	34
Mark 10:13-16	27
Mark 12:30-31	42
Mark 14:12-15	55
Mark 15:46—16:7	19
Mark 16:15	92
Luke 1:26-33	30
Luke 2:1-20	8
Luke 2:8-14	30
Luke 2:6-16	6
Luke 3:11	91
Luke 10:20b	22
Luke 18:22	70
Luke 22:39-43	30
Luke 23:55—24:7	18
John 1:29	40
John 3:16	35, 78, 86
John 10:1-5	46
John 10:30	62
John 11:25-26	45
John 12:12-13	16
John 13:35	98
John 14:26	75
John 14:27	43
John 15:12	67
Acts 1:8	39
Acts 2:1-17, 32-38, 41-42	21
Acts 2:38	31
Acts 11:26b	32
Acts 12:24	65
Romans 1:9b	44
Romans 3:20, 22a	85
Romans 8:28	74
Romans 10:9	81
Romans 12:13	56
Romans 15:4	77
1 Corinthians 13:13	68
2 Corinthians 5:15, 17	15
2 Corinthians 9:7	97
2 Corinthians 13:13	49
Ephesians 1:7a	37
Ephesians 1:23a	33
Ephesians 4:5-6	62
Ephesians 4:16	33
Ephesians 4:32	37
Ephesians 5:1	28
Colossians 3:12	58
1 Thessalonians 5:18	69
2 Timothy 3:16	78
Hebrews 1:14	30
Hebrews 11:1	36
Hebrews 13:16	73
1 John 1:9	13, 37, 63
1 John 2:1-2	17
1 John 3:11	26
Revelation 1:3a	79
Revelation 21:1-4	81